THE ULTIMATE CAMBRIDGE LAW TEST GUIDE

UniAdmissions

Published by RAR Medical Services Limited
www.uniadmissions.co.uk
info@uniadmissions.co.uk
Tel: +44 (0) 208 068 0438

ABOUT THE AUTHORS

Aiden graduated from Peterhouse, Cambridge, with a **First Class Honours Law degree** and has tutored Oxbridge law applicants at *UniAdmissions* for two years.

Aiden is a trainee solicitor at a top US firm in London. He has a keen interest in helping out students with application advice as he believes that students should get all the help they need in order to succeed in their applications. In his spare time, he likes to travel and run outdoors.

Rohan is the **Director of Operations** at *UniAdmissions* and is responsible for its technical and commercial arms. He graduated from Gonville and Caius College, Cambridge and is a fully qualified doctor. Over the last five years, he has tutored hundreds of successful Oxbridge and Medical applicants. He has also authored twenty books on admissions tests and interviews.

Rohan has taught physiology to undergraduates and interviewed medical school applicants for Cambridge. He has published research on bone physiology and writes education articles for the Independent and Huffington Post. In his spare time, Rohan enjoys playing the piano and table tennis.

THE ULTIMATE CAMBRIDGE LAW TEST GUIDE

AIDEN ANG
ROHAN AGARWAL

UniAdmissions

CONTENTS

THE BASICS

WHAT IS THE CLT?

The Cambridge Law Test (CLT) is a one-hour written exam for law students who are applying to the University of Cambridge. You have one hour to answer an essay-based question. You are not expected to have any pre-requisite knowledge of the law. You will be assessed based on your clarity of expression and how you interpret an essay question. The test is used as a further piece of information to assess a candidate's suitability for admission into Cambridge.

TEST STRUCTURE

You must choose one essay question out of three. It is typically a paper-based test, unless you have special circumstances. The test structure might differ if you are doing your interview overseas. Due to the COVID-19 Pandemic, the test was held online on the same date for all applicants in the 2021/22 admission cycle.

WHO HAS TO SIT FOR THE CLT?

Only candidates who have been shortlisted for the Cambridge Law Interview will be asked to sit for the test. It is generally done before your interview, subject to differences depending on which college you have applied for. For the 2021/22 admission cycle, the CLT was done online after the interview for international students who had interviews in November. For local students, the CLT was generally done prior to interview.

WHERE DO I SIT THE CLT?

It will generally be in the college which you will be interviewing in. If you have requested for an overseas interview, separate arrangements will be made. Your college will inform you accordingly.

WHY IS THE CLT USED?

The CLT was developed by University of Cambridge as an alternative to the LNAT to assess a candidate's suitability for reading law in Cambridge. Hence, students applying to read law in University of Cambridge will not need to sit the LNAT. The CLT differs from the LNAT as the CLT does not comprise a multiple-choice questions (MCQ) section. Candidates are only expected to write one essay question in an hour. The questions differ from Section B of the LNAT as the questions tend to skew more towards legal questions as opposed to general current affairs essay questions.

WHEN DO I SIT THE CLT?

You will be informed by the college you have applied to by email whether you are shortlisted for the interview. If you are, they will arrange your CLT accordingly, which is likely to take place before your interview. If you have applied for an interview overseas, separate arrangements will be made. Your college will inform you of the relevant dates and venue.

HOW MUCH DOES IT COST?

Taking the CLT is completely free; the college will arrange the test for you if you are shortlisted for interview.

CAN I RE-SIT THE CLT?

You will not be allowed to re-sit the CLT but if you are unsuccessful following the interview you can request for feedback to gauge how well you did in the CLT. This might help you should you wish to re-apply to Cambridge the following year.

IF I RE-APPLY, DO I HAVE TO RE-SIT THE CLT?

As mentioned above, if you re-apply to Cambridge, you will be asked to sit the CLT again.

WHEN DO I GET MY RESULTS?

If you are successful following the interview, you will generally not find out how well you did for the CLT. However, if you are unsuccessful, you can request feedback from the college which you applied to and they will tell you your score on the CLT.

HOW IS THE CLT SCORED?

The essay, like the interview, is scored on a scale of 1-10. 1 is the worst score and 10 is the best. Successful candidates will usually score at least a 7 to stand a good chance of being admitted. However, different colleges place different weight on the CLT and the colleges do not publicly reveal the weight they place on the CLT.

HOW IS THE CLT USED?

The University of Cambridge Faculty of Law website states that the Cambridge Law Test is only intended to complement the other elements of their admissions process. It will be considered alongside the interview, your personal statement and your grades to date.

HOW DOES MY SCORE COMPARE?

As mentioned above, successful candidates tend to score at least a 7 on a scale of 10. This is subject to how well you have done on your interview, how good your grades are and your personal statement.

ACCESS ARRANGEMENTS

If you require special circumstances such as extra time or a separate room, you should always arrange this with the college which you will be interviewing in beforehand. The college will contact you if you are shortlisted for interview and ask whether you require any special circumstances.

GENERAL ADVICE

PRACTICE

A good place to start will be to refer to this guide! Whilst it is stated that you do not need any prior knowledge of law to do the CLT, it is good to read up on the fundamental principles of law so that you start to think and write like a lawyer. This will also help you understand the more legalistic questions that the CLT tends to set. You should also look at our sample essays to differentiate a good essay from a bad one, before having a go at practicing a few essay titles so that you are confident and prepared on the day itself.

START EARLY

You should get into the habit of preparing early. A good way to start is to start a daily habit of reading legal news so that you are exposed to the kind of topics that tend to be asked in the CLT. There are plenty of news websites that provide free legal news, such as the law section of The Guardian and The Telegraph. If you have a subscription to The Financial Times or The Economist, they provide excellent legal news from time to time as well. You should also look at the law resources on the HE+ website as these are resources created and written by Cambridge students and academics.

HOW TO WORK

You should focus on reading as widely as possible about the law so that you will not be stumped by all the questions available to you during the actual test. They can be on very specific topics such as corporate manslaughter or intellectual property law. Whilst they do not expect you to have any prior knowledge of law, it helps if you have read up about such issues and have a general idea about the points you can raise.

You should look at our sample essays to learn how to best structure your essay in a succinct and cohesive manner. You should also practice writing essays under timed conditions so that you are able to produce a sufficiently detailed essay within one hour.

FOCUS ON TOPICS YOU ARE COMFORTABLE WITH

Since you only have to do one question out of three, you should have a more focused approach to your studying. You could pick a few topics you are comfortable and confident with. For example, if you have a strong interest in criminal law, you should focus on doing your research in that area. If a question relevant to criminal law comes out, you will be confident and well-prepared to answer it well. You cannot predict what three topics might come out therefore you should prepare more than just one topic. However, you should not be spending too much time on topics you have no interest in or struggle to understand – for example, if you do not understand company law and have no confidence in answering an essay question on it, it might be a better use of your time in focusing on other topics for the CLT.

MARKING

The CLT is marked on a scale of 1-10. The Faculty of Law Cambridge Law Test page provides a marking scheme for the CLT. It says essay marked a 7 is 'probably worth an offer'. Hence, candidates should strive for at least a 7 to stand a good chance of receiving an offer. The criteria stated in the marking scheme includes being able to: i) identify and engage with the issues raised by the question and to critically analyse and evaluate; ii) be clear in your writing; iii) explaining your reasons in a clear and logical manner; and iv) writing in a coherent, well-structured and balanced manner.

BOOKING YOUR TEST

As mentioned above, this is done for you by your college after you receive an interview invite.

SAMPLE QUESTIONS

There are five sample CLT papers freely available online:
https://resources.law.cam.ac.uk/documents/official/clt_sample_tests.pdf

TIME MANAGEMENT

An hour passes by quickly and you should plan your time wisely. Whilst it is tempting to jump straight to answering a question the moment the test starts, you run the huge risk of not reading the question properly, or not having a proper plan in mind.

Remember – you are not marked solely based on your content alone. Structure is, in many ways, more important than your content. A good structure enables the marker to follow your arguments and this plays a big part in differentiating between a good essay worth 7 or more!

Take at least ten minutes at the start to properly plan your essay, especially your introduction and conclusion. The marker will be reading many of these essays. A strong introduction and conclusion can make up for a weak essay! An ideal introduction will set out clearly the points you will be making and direct the examiner accordingly instead of leaving them to guess what your argument is.

One final point is that it is better to have a shorter essay that is clear and to the point than a longer essay that is confusing and all over the place – quality over quantity!

BASIC CONCEPTS IN LAW

COMMON LAW VS. CIVIL LAW

England and Wales are under the common law system. This means that statutes (law implemented by Parliament) are heavily supplemented by judge-made law (decisions handed down by judges in the courts that are binding). There may be some areas of law that are largely determined by statute, for example company law. There are other areas of law that are almost solely based on common law, such as the law of murder. Besides England and Wales, there are many countries that adopt a similar common law approach such as Canada, India, Hong Kong and Singapore.

This can be contrasted to civil law, which is largely determined by codes (the equivalent of statutes in common law). This can be seen in the European countries and other large countries such as China and Japan. Judges are bound to adhere to the code and the decisions they make are not binding to the same extent as decisions made by judges in common law systems. The advantage of a civil law system is possibly more consistency and certainty. Judges are always bound by the civil code and are not allowed to change the law to a large extent. Under common law, judges have a lot more flexibility and power to use their discretion to change the law. The system of binding decisions means that they are easily able to adapt to novel situations and move on with the times.

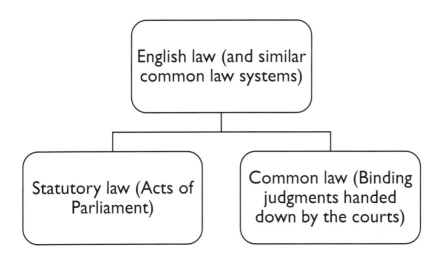

THE DIFFERENT LAW SUBJECTS

In a law degree, you will be expected to study the seven core subjects of law. These are considered the core areas of English law. All law students in the UK are currently expected to study Criminal Law, Tort Law, Constitutional/Public Law, Contract Law, Land/Property Law, Equity/Trust Law and EU Law.

Besides the core subjects, there are several other subjects that you can do in the law degree according to your interests. This is what makes doing a law degree exciting as you get to specialise in specific areas of law that you find interesting. At Cambridge, you can currently pick three optional papers in your second and third year.

Year	Subjects
1	Criminal, Tort, Roman, Constitutional
2	Contract, Land, Option 1, Option 2, Option 3
3	Equity, EU, Option 1, Option 2, Option 3/ Dissertation

These subjects can range from the more theoretical ones such as jurisprudence, criminology and legal history, to more practical and commercial ones such as company law, commercial law and civil procedure.

In addition, you are also able to select the option of doing a dissertation instead of paper in your final year. You can write a dissertation on a wide range of topics that may suit your preference, such as a family law dissertation on adoption or an international law dissertation on use of force.

CRIMINAL LAW

This is an area of law that receives the most publicity and hence most students will think they know something about. However, this is also one of the most complex, controversial, perplexing and confusing areas of law. There are also many related areas to criminal law that are considered separate domains. For example, Criminal Procedure and Evidence which deals with procedure and Criminology, Sentencing and the Penal System which deals more with crime and sentencing (both are taught as separate subjects in Cambridge).

There are certain hot topics that are heavily debated in the public arena, such as euthanasia (the right to die), joint enterprise (when two or more people are involved in the same crime) and historic sexual abuse cases. These are areas that are usually picked up by students. They are areas of contention because they appear on the news and raise countless ethical and theoretical questions. There are also several other academic areas of criminal law that have caused debate, such as defences (should being drunk be a defence to a crime) and recklessness.

A core tenet of criminal law is that in order for an accused to be convicted of a crime, it must be proved by the prosecution beyond reasonable doubt that he or she had the requisite actus reus (the physical action of the crime, such as the physical act of stealing a wallet). This must be accompanied by the requisite mens rea (the mental element – e.g. the intention of stealing the wallet). The accused will be allowed to raise a defence, for example the defence of lack of mens rea (the accused accidentally took the wallet without the intention of stealing it).

For certain crimes such as murder, it may be a defence to show that the accused killed the victim out of self-defence. There are also full defences and partial defences. You should read the Criminal chapter in "What About Law?" and look at the resources on HE+.

TORT LAW

Tort Law feels more unfamiliar to those who have not studied law but is more relevant to us than criminal law in our day-to-day life. Tort cases are civil cases – this is not to be confused with the difference between common law and civil law. In this case civil cases refer to private disputes that do not involve the state. Hence, a private party (people like you and I) sues another private party in tort, instead of a prosecutor (representing the state) bringing proceedings against a defendant (a criminal). This is why criminal cases are almost always named as 'R v. The Defendant', with 'R' referring to the Crown, whereas tort cases are just between two private parties.

In criminal law, where a defendant loses a case he or she will get a penal sentence, a fine, or a community sentence in general. Whereas in tort cases the losing party will usually be ordered to pay damages (compensation) or be ordered to refrain from doing a particular act such as under an injunction.

Tort cases are generally civil duties that fall outside the realm of contract law. This means that there was no contract between the two parties. For example, in the situation where you were applying to Cambridge and needed a reference from your teacher, the teacher is under an implied duty of care. The teacher should provide an accurate reference for you (he or she is however under no duty to boost your achievements if it is not reflective of your actual achievements!).

If a teacher negligently fails to provide an accurate reference, there *might* be a possible tortious claim. For example, a teacher could have mistook you for another student that was always skipping class and gave you a bad reference you failed to get a place in Cambridge. However, this is subject to the different steps involved in a tortious claim.

The general steps involved in establishing a claim in tort are as follows: i) Duty of care – does the defendant owe a duty of care to the claimant; ii) Breach – has the duty been breach; iii) Causation – was the claimant's loss caused by the defendant's breach; and iv) Loss – has the defendant suffered loss as a result of the breach.

Duty of care
A duty of care can be implied from a relationship: professional relationship between solicitor to client, relationship of trust and confidence between teacher and student, employer and employee. The courts will usually look at the circumstances of the case and decide whether the relationship between the claimant and defendant shows that a duty of care is owed by the defendant. In the example, there is a relationship between the student and teacher.

Breach
It must be shown that the duty of care owed has been breached by the defendant. For example, if a defendant performed his or her job negligently (carelessly) and failed to reach the standard expected of a reasonable professional in the same industry. This will establish that the duty of care has been breached. In our example, the teacher breached their duty by failing to provide an accurate reference.

Causation

Further, it must be shown that it was the breach that has caused the loss to the claimant. Using the example given above, the student might still would not have gotten into Cambridge despite the wrongly given reference. The student may have done poorly in the interview or the CLT. Even if the reference was spotless the student still would not have been admitted. Then, causation would not have been established and a claim will not be available. Sometimes, there might be an intervening cause that breaks the causative chain. For example, if the student contracted an illness that impeded his or her performance at the interview, the bad reference will no longer be the causative element behind the unsuccessful outcome.

Loss

Finally, loss must be established for a claim to exist. In some cases, this is straightforward, such as losing a certain amount of money as a result of the negligence of your solicitor. In other cases, such as the example used above, this might be harder to assess – how do we assess the loss of failing to get into Cambridge in monetary terms? Usually claimants will argue this point in terms of loss of future earnings, such as arguing that failing to get into Cambridge will lead to a loss of future job prospects. This is a very controversial area in tort law. The assessment of loss usually boils down to very subjective and speculative judgments.

You should read the Tort chapter in "What About Law?" and look at the resources on HE+.

CONSTITUTIONAL/PUBLIC LAW

A recent big constitutional case would be the Brexit decision handed down by the Supreme Court, which was an application brought on behalf of Gina Miller. Constitutional law plays a big part in upholding values such as the rule of law, preserving human rights and ensuring that the government does not abuse its powers. Some of these principles may seem really abstract but they play an important role in making England an attractive place to live and do business because of the strong rule of law. If you are interested in this area of law, a good introductory book is The Rule of Law by Tom Bingham.

One peculiarity of England is that we lack a written constitution. Instead, our 'constitution' is in multiple different documents and principles. This is unlike many other countries like the US where they have a written constitution that takes an onerous process to amend. There have been countless debates about whether the unwritten constitution works or whether we should adopt a written constitution, and this is where things start to get highly abstract and theoretical at times. This is an important concept to understand as it could and has been the subject of sample essay CLT questions.

Due to the lack of a written constitution, judges tend to determine what our constitutional rights are from a variety of sources. These include established practices, certain treaties and articles that set out fundamental rights such as the European Convention on Human Rights (ECHR)) or international treaties such as the Geneva Convention. Human rights are a big part of constitutional law. This has been governed largely by the Human Rights Act 1998 (HRA 1998). However, it has been proposed that this will be repealed and replaced with a Bill of Rights following the Brexit vote as the HRA was largely implemented as a result of the entry into the EU.

CONTRACT LAW

Contract Law is arguably one of the most important subjects in the commercial world. This is because almost every transaction or agreement these days involves bilateral or multilateral contracts. It is fundamental for a particular jurisdiction to provide strong, consistent contract law principles so that commercial entities can conduct business with certainty and the top business hubs in the world will tend to have very well-established contract law principles, such as New York and London.

Contract and Tort are intertwined, with many cases involve a concurrent claim in both contract and tort. For example, a claimant might sue a defendant for breach of contract and sue the same defendant for breach of duty of care. It is important to note that a contractual claim will ever only exist if there is an express or implied term.

An express term is straightforward – you can usually identify a contractual clause that gives effect to a duty or obligation. An implied term is where it gets more complicated. If there is no express written term of a contract, will the courts imply a term based on the conduct of the parties?

For example, if one party was a skilled professional, will there be an implied term that he or she had to act with reasonable care and skill? Alternatively, if a contract was very badly drafted and it is unclear where there is a particular obligation or duty to perform a certain act, will the courts imply a term into the contract based on necessity, custom or business efficacy?

This is an area that has sparked immense academic debate. There is a fine balancing act between achieving justice to a party by making contract law more flexible and ensuring that contract law provides certainty and finality so that businesses feel comfortable being subject to the contract laws of a particular jurisdiction.

Another area of contract law that has resulted in endless academic debate is the English concept of 'consideration'. In English law, it is held that for a contract to be valid and enforceable there should always be sufficient consideration. This has been interpreted as widely to include returning a chocolate wrapper to the manufacturer. The wrapper might be seemingly worthless, but this constitutes sufficient consideration because the company benefited from the publicity. This is an area of law that has provided a lot of uncertainty and there has been calls to follow other jurisdictions in abolishing the doctrine of consideration and replace it with principles that are easier to understand.

LAND/PROPERTY LAW

This area of law affects a range of people: from students renting an apartment to multi-billion mega commercial properties such as landmark buildings in London. The reason why land is so valuable is because land is a finite resource – there is only so much land you can build properties on.

In order to maximise the value of land, several different forms of rights have been created under land law in order to allow land to be utilised to the fullest. Therefore, land law is regularly interspersed with equitable doctrines.

For example, Person A may be a legal owner of a plot of land but Person B may be the beneficial owner. The person who owns the land and has their name registered in the land title will be the legal owner. They have the strongest, indefeasible right over the property. If this person was holding the property on trust for another person, the other person will have a beneficial right to the property. For example, a father might wish to pass down the property to his son when the son becomes of age.

On this same plot of land, there may also be a Person C with an equitable interest and Person D with have possessory title. Most properties are purchased with the help of a mortgage; hence the bank will usually have a legal proprietary interest in the land, but if the mortgage was not executed correctly the bank might nevertheless still have an equitable proprietary interest.

Lastly, if the father decided to rent out the property to a student, the student will have a possessory title in the form of a right to occupy the property during the duration of the rental agreement. This is a complex area of law that involves many equitable principles.

Another interesting and controversial concept is adverse possession. If a squatter lived in a property for a requisite number of years without the owner objecting, the squatter may obtain a right to occupy the property. This may seem counter-intuitive to the idea of land law protecting the rights of owners, but it's deemed as a way of ensuring that land is utilised to the fullest. It also involves human rights issues, especially when a person may have developed a right to family life in a house.

Finally, the land registry has also provided interesting discussion, especially when there is an emphasis on finality of title and certainty of rights in land law. This provides landowners and commercial property investors with confidence in the law. The idea is that any rights in land should be recorded in the land registry and the land registry will provide indisputable evidence of a person's right to the land. This forms a parallel with the main idea behind contract law; finality and certainty is desirable but to what extent should the law be flexible to achieve justice and fairness in certain special cases?

EQUITY/TRUST LAW

You may have come across tax havens, trust funds, and big charities in the news - a lot of these has to do with equity and trust law. This area of law is notoriously abstract and complicated.

Equity has a long historical baggage and the courts of the common law and equity used to be separated. A good description of the relationship between equity and the common law would be that equity exists to supplement common law principles and help them achieve justice and fairness. In modern day, judges use equitable principles to provide flexibility while applying the common law which can be rigid. The chapter on Equity in "What About Law" will be useful in helping you understand the basic idea behind equity. As it is a tough area, it is unlikely that many (or any) CLT questions will be set on this topic.

The two well-known equitable doctrines are: i) Equity does not help those that do not come with clean hands and ii) Equity will not act in vain. When deciding a case that involves an equitable remedy being available, the courts will tend to have regard to the equitable doctrines. Equitable remedies include rescission of a contract or granting an injunction.

The claimant 'did not come with clean hands' if the claimant was partly to be blamed for the negative outcome, therefore the courts may be less-inclined to grant an equitable remedy. If granting a remedy will result in no difference, the courts will not grant an injunction to prevent the defendant from releasing the information since 'equity will not act in vain' and granting the remedy will not make a difference. For example, a trade secret had already been leaked to the public.

Trust law provides for sophisticated mechanisms such as being able to establish an offshore company. This helps reduce a company's tax liability as well as being able to set up a trust fund to benefit one's child.

The basic idea behind trust law is that you can separate the legal and beneficial interest behind an asset (sum of cash or a property). This is so that the legal owner can hold the property on trust for the beneficiary. The legal owner will exercise control over the property while holding on to it for the beneficiary. An example of such a relationship would be an asset manager investing in the funds on behalf of the client. The beneficiary, having an equitable proprietary interest, will be able to rely on certain remedies if the legal owner mishandles the property in bad faith.

EU LAW

This area of law that has been the subject of endless media coverage due to the recent Brexit vote. This area of law is very easily misunderstood by the general public. The 'Remain' team tend to accuse the 'Leave' team of failing to understand the mechanics behind EU law and being misled by politicians. This is where you can form your own informed opinion after having a better understanding of the structure and function of EU law.

EU law is considered a superior law to English law after UK's entry into the EU, due to the European Communities Act 1972 where a seminal constitutional case by the House of Lords held that the UK has submitted itself to the supremacy of EU law. This means that EU law triumphs over English law and this is perhaps why most Leave voters would argue that the UK has lost its sovereignty and right to legislate.

However, the mechanics and structure behind EU law is a lot more sophisticated and layered than that. Under EU law there is the notion of conferral, subsidiarity and proportionality. What this means is that there are certain areas of laws where member states of the EU have the exclusive right to legislate on behalf of their own nation, such as in areas of defence and security.

There are other areas where competence is 'shared'. For example, in areas of health and safety, member states are free to legislate provided the EU has not already laid down common rules. The doctrine of proportionality also ensures that member states will not be held liable for failing to legislate in accordance with EU law unless they fail the proportionality test. Therefore, despite EU law being supreme, there are many areas of laws, especially crucial and sensitive areas that are reserved for the member states to legislate.

The main tenets of EU law, besides the constitutional principles mentioned above, are the freedom of movement of goods and persons. This has been extremely controversial, especially with regards to the free movement of persons. The Leave voters have argued that this has led to uncontrolled mass migration. The idea behind free movement of goods and persons is to promote economic interdependence and to allow artificial barriers to entry to be removed. This promotes the economic growth and distribution of talent amongst the different member states. Whether this is a successful or failing project involves a lot of political debate, but it is the role of a law student or a legal academic to focus on the legalistic issues and form an objective viewpoint instead of being too muddled over the political side of EU law.

CASE LAW

Why is case law important?
Under the English common law system, judgments handed down by the higher courts play a crucial role in shaping the law due to the doctrine of *stare decisis* (where judgments handed down by the higher courts are binding on the lower courts in general).

Hence, the many cases handed down by the judges every year serve precedential value. The role of a law student and a lawyer is to analyse what the case establishes (the *ratio* of the case). It is also to extract relevant legal principles that can be derived from what the judges say.

For example, a judge may make a remark that is technically non-binding (an *obiter* remark). However, such a remark may serve as a guide for future legal cases. Furthermore, judges frequently do not come into a unanimous decision. The dissenting judgments are sometimes worth a read as well, especially when the judges make interesting arguments against the majority and there are situations where these dissenting arguments are upheld in subsequent cases.

For the CLT, they do not expect you to be reading or referencing cases (you do this in law school). On the other hand, it would be helpful to read the resources on HE+ which structure the different arguments behind certain cases in a helpful and introductory way.

This would help you understand how to build and structure your arguments in your essay. English law is broadly made up of two main sources. From the diagram above, you can see that case law is created by judges and statutory law is created by the Parliament. There is also the government which is the executive. Together, these three entities form the overriding infrastructure of the law and act collaboratively in order to implement, enact and enforce the law.

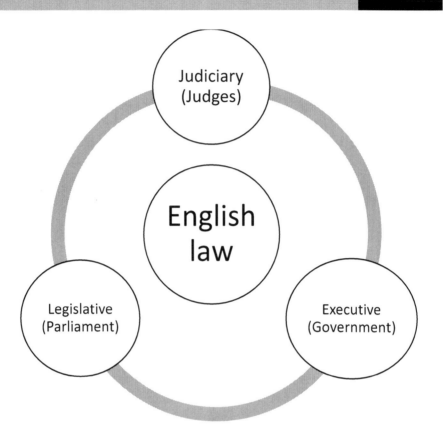

We have included examples of some well-known cases that are worth a read. Be mindful however that this list is nowhere near exhaustive and you have been warned that law is a subject that involves a lot of reading, partly because there can be thousands of cases for each subject!

Donoghue v Stevenson (Tort)

This is perhaps one of the most well-known cases for law students, partly due to its unique facts and because of its subsequent importance in tort.

What the case established
Donoghue v Stevenson held that manufacturers could owe a duty of care to consumers under negligence in tort even if the consumer and the manufacturer did not have a formal contract (and hence no contractual claim is available).

Facts of the case
The claimant bought a bottle of ginger beer from the defendant, who was a manufacturer of ginger beers. When the claimant drank the bottle of ginger beer, she claimed that there was a snail in the bottle which made her sick as a result.

What the judge(s) said
Lord Atkin famously introduced the 'neighbour principle' in this case, stating that 'the rule that you must love your neighbour became in law that you must not injure your neighbour'. He further held that 'you must take reasonable care to avoid acts or omissions which you could reasonably foresee would be likely to injure your neighbour'. With regards to whom can be regarded as your neighbour, he mentioned that this 'seemed to be persons who were so closely and directly affected by your act that you ought reasonably to have them in contemplation as being so affected when you directed your mind to the acts or omissions which were called into question'.

Why is this case important?
This case resulted in the development of the concept of negligence under tort law, where a duty of care can be established under the 'neighbour principle'. This allowed certain claimants to bring a potential claim under tort for damages they have suffered, which proved particularly useful especially when they could not bring a contractual claim due to a lack of contract.

Therefore, a manufacturer could owe a duty of care if they could reasonably foresee that consumers would likely be injured if they were negligent in producing their ginger beers. Consumers fell under the definition of a 'neighbour' as they were so closely and directly affected by the act of the manufacturer that the manufacturer ought to reasonably have the consumers in contemplation as being potentially affected when they thought about their act in question. In simpler terms, the manufacturer should have had known that consumers would be affected by their product.

The current state of the law
Tort provides protection for consumers when a contract fails to provide adequate protection in the form of an express clause. For example, there is an implied term in tort to provide reasonable care and skill in the provision of services, such as when a solicitor provides a professional service to a client. There is also an implied term that goods produced must be fit for purpose, hence suppliers must ensure that the goods they supply are fit for the purpose that the consumer is going to use them for.

Caparo Industries Plc v Dickman (Tort)

This case further developed the law of negligence and introduced further elements needed for a duty of care to be established.

What the case established
The case held that for a duty of care to be found, three elements must be fulfilled: (1) there must be an adequate degree of proximity in the parties' relationship, (2) it must be in the contemplation of the parties that a report was needed in order to enter into the transaction and (3) the claimant must have placed reliance on the report in deciding whether or not to enter into the transaction.

Facts of the case
The claimant sought to establish that the defendant, an accounting firm, owed a duty of care to them when preparing an auditor's report as required by statute. The claimant held that there was a negligent misstatement since they bought shares in reliance on the report. Therefore, they suffered a loss as a result of the negligent misstatement.

What the judge(s) said
It was held that the defendant did not owe the claimant any duty of care. The defendant, as auditors of a public company, regularly prepared accounts as part of their job scope. This was held in contrast to the preparation of a specific report for a specific company. The defendant did not owe a general duty to the public who might have relied on their report when entering an investment. The judges further held that to impose such a liability would 'open the floodgates' as the defendant's liability will be to an indiscriminate pool of people.

Why is this case important?
This case further expanded the test for a duty of care in tort beyond the 'neighbour principle' that was established in *Donoghue v Stevenson,* to include the three elements that need to be established before a duty of care is established. Furthermore, the judges also introduced the important concept of restricting economic loss in the absence of a contractual relationship. This is in the interest of commercial certainty that commercial entities can predict the extent of their loss and are not subject to potential enormous losses under tort.

The current state of the law
Tort provides an additional layer of protection for consumers in the form of implied terms and providing an avenue for compensation in the absence of a contract. However, the law arguably provides less protection for sophisticated commercial parties. Such parties are expected to protect their rights under contract and in the absence of a contractual right, any potential claim under tort will be limited to the extent that a duty of care will only be established if the onerous test under *Caparo Industries plc v Dickman* is fulfilled.

R v Brown (Criminal)

This is a very interesting case that is particularly infamous amongst law students due to its facts. However, this case also laid down an important principle regarding when someone can consent to harm. It would also be useful to read the commentary and analysis on this case in What About Law.

What the case established
In law, consent can be a defence in certain circumstances. The case held that a victim cannot consent to harm for acts which causes serious harm except for when they fall within certain recognised categories (sports) or there exist good policy reasons. In this case, the satisfying of sado-masochistic desires did not constitute as a 'good reason' for such consent to be valid.

Facts of the case
A group of sado-masochists engaged in consensual acts of violence against each other for sexual gratification and were accordingly charged with various offences under the Offences Against the Person Act 1861 as the victims suffered physical harm as a result of the sexual acts.

What the judge(s) said
The majority of the judges held that it was not in the public interest that a person is allowed to seriously wound another for no good reason; without such a reason, the victim's consent would not be a defence to a charge under the relevant sections of the Offences Against the Person Act 1861. Furthermore, the majority held that the satisfying of sado-masochistic desires did not constitute a good reason.

Why is this case important?
This case sparked immense controversy and the difference in judgment between the majority and minority showed a huge difference in attitude towards whether someone can consent to harmful sexual activity. The majority held that one will not be allowed to consent to such harm as it would be against the 'public interest'. The minority was less convinced and said that we should not rule out consent for such sexual activity provided that the consent given was valid.

The majority decision was thus the much more conservative decision. Academics have argued that the judges should not act as a 'morality police' and disallow individuals from performing certain sexual acts even if both parties are willing and have consented to it. A parallel has been drawn to other 'harmful' activities that can be consented to such as tattooing and body modifications.

The current state of the law
A victim is not allowed to consent to harm that is not 'merely transient and trifling'. This area of law is controversial because it was held in another case that an old married couple was allowed to brandish the husband's initials on the wife's buttocks because it had 'sentimental value' and was not against the public interest *(R v Wilson)*. Academics have argued that this shows a moral double standard.

R v Jogee (Criminal)

This is a more recent case (2016 Supreme Court decision) that changed the law regarding joint enterprise and secondary liability (where two or more people are involved in the same offence).

What the case established
This case reversed the previous decision laid down by the Privy Council (a court that handles cases involving British colonies) and held that it is not enough to find a secondary party responsible when that secondary party merely foresaw the possibility that the primary offender would have acted the way that he or she did.

Facts of the case
This Supreme Court decision involved an appeal regarding a conviction for murder involving two individuals – the main issue was whether a secondary party who did not kill the victim could be liable for murder merely by foreseeing the possibility that the primary defendant would have acted the way that he did.

What the judge(s) said
The judges thought that the law of murder required a low mental element of 'intention to cause serious injury, without intent to kill or to cause risk to life'. Hence, the old Privy Council principle that extended liability to a secondary party based on mere foresight was unsatisfactory. This was because having the mere foresight that the principal may commit murder further lowered the threshold required to establish the mental element for murder. This also created an unorthodox situation where a lower mental element was required for the secondary party as opposed to the principal.

Why is this case important?
The law regarding joint enterprise and secondary liability has always been muddled and this case provided much needed clarity regarding the position of the law. It may be desirable for the secondary to be liable for the same offence is because they can be equally culpable as the principal at times. However, it was not desirable for the law to create an illogical situation where the mental element required for the secondary party to be liable for murder was lower than what was required from the principal. Hence, this case restored the position where the foreseeability of the principal committing the murder will not alone be enough for the mental element of murder to be established for the secondary party, although it can provide strong evidence.

The current state of the law
When a secondary party is involved in an offence with the principal, the mere foreseeability that the principal will commit the crime is not alone by itself be enough for the secondary party to be liable for the same offence.

R. (on the application of Miller) v Secretary of State for Exiting the European Union (Constitutional)

This is another very recent Supreme Court decision and possibly one of the most well-known one. This is due to the immense press coverage it received ever since the Brexit referendum happened. For a better understanding on how EU law and English law interrelate, read the chapter on EU law in "What About Law".

What the case established
The Supreme Court, perhaps controversially, held that the Government did not have the necessary power under the royal prerogative to give notice pursuant to TEU Art 50(2) for the UK to withdraw from the EU. The Supreme Court held that an Act of Parliament will be required.

Facts of the case
This decision went up to the Supreme Court when Gina Miller challenged the legality of the government giving a formal notice under Art 50 to leave the EU. This decision raised important constitutional questions regarding the separation of powers between the legislative, executive and judiciary.

What the judge(s) said
The judges reiterated that the European Communities Act 1972 (ECA) formally introduced EU law into English law. It established EU law as a supreme overriding source of domestic law.

It was envisaged that any new obligations or rights were only implemented in English law following a variation of the definition of 'Treaties' under the ECA. Hence, the judges held that the Parliament could not have intended that the ECA would continue to bring in new EU law rights if the UK was no longer under the control of EU law.

Hence, it was not envisaged that the royal prerogative could bring an end to the UK's legal obligations under EU law. If the UK leaves the EU, they would no longer be bound under EU law – this signifies a major constitutional amendment. The judges stressed that it would be inconsistent with the fundamental principle of parliamentary sovereignty for such a constitutional change to be brought about by the royal prerogative, i.e., executive action alone. This is especially so when it was Parliament which decided that EU law should be granted supreme status over English law in the first place.

Hence, the judges concluded that the royal prerogative power exists solely in the international law plane and could not be used to alter a fundamental constitutional right without statutory intervention.

Why is this case important?
This case plays a hugely important role in setting out what the constitutional law dictates in an unprecedented situation. It makes it clear that the doctrine of separation of powers should be respected and the executive cannot solely implement a decision that would impinge on the legislative's domain. Since the legislative (Parliament) was the one that introduced the supreme status of EU law into English law in the first place, statutory intervention is needed in order to remove such a status from English law and the royal prerogative alone is not enough to introduce such a fundamental constitutional change.

The current state of the law
Again, this is an unprecedented situation. This case hopefully sets a precedence for any subsequent events involving the use of the royal prerogative. This means that the executive (the government) will not be allowed to exercise their powers to implement a fundamental constitutional amendment in the absence of statutory intervention.

Associated Provincial Picture Houses Ltd v Wednesbury Corp (Constitutional)

This is an important, albeit old constitutional law case which established the 'Wednesbury principle', allowing the courts to hold that a public authority has acted 'so unreasonably that no reasonable public authority would make such a decision'.

This principle has been used to determine when a public authority can be held liable for acting unreasonably, such as a government agency dealing with an applicant's case for asylum.

What the case established
It was held that where a public authority makes a decision and has taken into account what they ought to take into account, the court could nevertheless interfere with their decision if 'it was so unreasonable that no reasonable authority could ever have come to it'.

Facts of the case
The claimant, a cinema proprietor, argued that a condition imposed by the defendant, a local licensing authority, was outside the scope of their powers. The condition related to the grant of permission for Sunday performances at the cinema.

The local authority had the power under statutory law to grant licences for cinema performances. This licence was subject to conditions imposed by the authority. The local authority issued a ban on children under 15 from entering the cinema due to their health and well-being.

What the judge(s) said
The court held that it could scrutinise the local authority's decision to determine whether they have considered matters which they ought to have considered and have fulfilled their respective duty.

Hence, the court has a power over the local authority to the extent that the court can police whether the local authority has overstepped its boundary and acted *ultra vires* (outside its powers). This provides an important check and balance against the public authority to ensure that they do not abuse their powers. In the *Wednesbury* case itself, it was held that the local authority acted reasonably in imposing the ban.

Why is this case important?
This case is important mainly for establishing the *Wednesbury* unreasonable test. This has been used subsequently in numerous constitutional and administrative law cases. This is used to determine whether a public authority or a branch of the executive/government can be held liable for failing to consider matters when arriving at a decision. This enhances the judiciary's role as a check and balance against the decisions implemented by the executive and prevents an abuse of power situation which leads to the applicant suffering damage.

The current state of the law
The courts have an overall power of declaring that a public authority has acted unreasonably. However, this is not an all-encompassing overriding power. The courts cannot substitute the public authority's decision for their own decision. The courts can only determine in specific situations when a public authority has acted outside of their powers (*ultra vires*) in failing to consider certain key facts or issues that are pertinent to the relevant case in hand.

Carlill v Carbolic Smoke Ball Co (Contract)

This is an extremely old case (1893) that dealt with whether an advertisement put up by a store can be constituted as an 'offer' in a contract. This is a reminder that even though the law is constantly developing and changing, sometimes legal principles can be traced back to cases or statutory law in the 1800s!

What the case established
It was held that an advertisement could constitute an offer to everyone, which meant that anyone could accept the offer if they fulfilled the conditions stated. It was also held that the customer would not need to signify his or her intention to accept the offer for there to be a valid acceptance of offer if the customer has fulfilled the necessary condition.

Facts of the case
The company involved was a manufacturer of a certain 'medicine' named the 'carbolic smoke ball', which was supposed to prevent someone from catching a flu. The company went on to publish an advertisement in the newspaper claiming that anyone will be entitled to £100 if they caught the flu whilst using the smoke ball three times a day for two weeks. They also had to follow the specific instructions set out by the usage of the ball. The advertisement stated that the company has deposited £1,000 with a bank to show their sincerity in making the offer.

A customer purchased the ball after reading this advertisement and did catch a flu whilst using the ball. The company tried to argue that this was not a valid contractual offer as it was worded way too vaguely. It was offered to 'anyone in the world' and did not stipulate a stop date. The company also further argued that the customer failed to signify their intention to accept the offer and hence there was no valid acceptance even if there was an offer.

What the judge(s) said

The judges held that the advertisement should not have been considered something now referred to as a 'mere puff'. A 'mere puff' refers to a kind of statement that was not intended to be an offer and non-binding. Here, the company had shown intention to be legally bound by depositing money in the bank. It had meant for the statement to be an offer and an offer restricted to those who acted upon the terms contained in the advertisement.

Even though the general rule was that for an acceptance of an offer to be binding the offeree had to signal his or her intention of accepting the offer, this was an exception. The offer was unilateral (offeror bound as soon as a specific act is performed) therefore the condition that the offeree had to show an express consent to be bound by the offer was waived. In this case the company was bound once the customer performed the stated conditions.

Why is this case important?

This early case established the fact that an advertisement can be constituted as a valid offer of a contract and will not be a 'mere puff', hence advertisers have to be careful not to create a binding contract by making certain promises in their advertisements. Furthermore, this case also nicely sets out the different elements behind the establishment of a contract – offer, acceptance, consideration and intention to be bound by the contract.

The current state of the law

An advertisement can constitute a binding offer of a contract provided that the other elements of a contractual claim are established – namely a valid acceptance, consideration as well as an intention to be bound by the contract.

Hadley v Baxendale (Contract)

This is another very old case that establishes the principle of remoteness behind contractual claims, hence providing a sensible limit with what can be claimed as damages under a contract.

What the case established
This case established the principle of remoteness that has been frequently cited and applied in subsequent contract cases. It was established that the damages that can be claimed from a breach of contract should be fair and reasonable and must be held to have arose naturally from the breach of a contract and should have been in the contemplation of the parties when the contract was made.

Facts of the case
The claimant was a mill owner, and the defendant was a manufacturer of a shaft used in the mill. The claimant needed a new shaft for its steam engine for its mill to work. Hence, they contacted the defendant to supply a new one. The claimant told the defendant that they needed it immediately and the defendant hence promised to deliver it the very next day. However, the defendant was not aware that the mill would not work without a new shaft.

The defendant ended up taking several days to deliver the shaft. The claimant alleged that the defendant's negligence resulted in their mill being unworkable for a few days. The claimant sought damages to recover their loss of earnings and wages as a result of the defendant's negligence. The defendant argued that the damages being sought were too remote.

What the judge(s) said
The judges held that for damages to be recoverable under a contractual claim, it should be fair and reasonable and have arisen naturally from the breach of the contractual duty.

Furthermore, it should have been within the parties' contemplation when the contract was made that such a breach would result in the loss claimed. If there were any special circumstances present which one party has already informed the other party about, it would be held that the damages resulting from the breach would have been in the contemplation of the parties.

However, if the circumstances were not known by one of the parties, it cannot be held that the loss was in the contemplation of the parties. In this case, the defendant was not informed that the mill would be unworkable as a result of the missing shaft. As a result, the claim was held to be too remote and not within the parties' contemplation.

Why is this case important?
This case establishes the important principle of remoteness which is used to limit damages that can potentially be claimed under a contractual claim to the point where only damages that are reasonably in the contemplation of the parties when the contract was made can be claimed. This case has been regularly cited in subsequent cases involving assessing damages flowing from a breach of contract.

The current state of the law
Damages are limited by the remoteness principle and if there are special circumstances in a particular case, it should be communicated to the other party so that it will be in the contemplation of the parties that such a loss might result from a breach when the contract was made.

Jones v Kernott (Land/Family/Equity)

This case established a presumption that it was intended for the shared home to be divided equally between a couple subject to evidence indicating the contrary. This is also one of the cases which span many different subjects in law and includes an important judgment by Lady Hale which has provided stronger protection for women in family law situations.

What the case established

It was held that when (1) a house was bought in the joint names of a cohabiting couple, (2) they both contributed to the mortgage but (3) did not expressly declare their respective beneficial interests in the house, a presumption would arise. It would be presumed that their beneficial interests would reflect their legal interests (which in this case is 50-50 if they own the house jointly as cohabitants). This is subject to evidence to the contrary. It is the court's role to decide upon the evidence what is fair and just having regard to all the circumstances of the case.

Facts of the case

The parties bought the house in their joint names and took out a mortgage together in their joint names. They lived together as cohabitants and both contributed to the household expenses until Kernott moved out. Jones remained in the property with her children and started to pay the household expenses herself. Kernott stopped making anymore contributions. This continued for more than 14 years until the property was put up for sale. It was declared that Jones owned 90% of the property beneficially whilst Kernott was only entitled to a 10% beneficial interest. Kernott applied to the court to challenge this decision.

What the judge(s) said

The judges held that the starting point is that there is a presumption that the beneficial interests of the cohabitants will coincide with their legal interest. Since they owned the property as joint tenants, this means their beneficial interest would presumably be 50-50. However, this presumption can be rebutted based on the evidence available. Strong evidence would be if the parties did not contribute equally to the purchase of the property. The courts will try to assess what the parties' common intention was and how they intended to own the property.

The court placed a heavy emphasis that the presumption should be not rebutted easily. The decision to purchase the property in joint names signify an emotional and economic attachment to a couple's trusting relationship. If it was impossible to infer a common intention, the courts might resort to imputing an intention to the parties if it is fair and just in the circumstances. The courts decided that there was an intention to differ from the presumption in this case and the 90-10 split was accurate.

Why is this case important?
This case helps to protect the weaker party in a relationship. For example, it would afford protection in a situation where a matrimonial house is purchased together in a relationship and the relationship subsequently breaks down. The weaker party can raise the presumption that the house was meant to be shared equally when they were in a stable, loving relationship, especially if it was bought in the joint names of the couple.

The current state of the law
This decision provides a bit more protection for cohabitants in the event of a breakdown of their relationship. Cohabitants do not enjoy the same level of legal protection as married couples or civil partners. The weaker party often suffers as a result of a breakdown of relationship in the absence of any legal protection.

Re A (Conjoined Twins) (Family/Criminal)

This is a highly interesting case involving whether medical practitioners can separate a pair of conjoined twins if doing so would save the life of one of the twins but kill the other. If they were not separated, both twins would eventually die as one of the twins was weakening the life force of the other twin. You can also read about this case on HE+.

What the case established
This case established the defence of necessity in murder. The doctor was able to raise the defence that murder was necessary to save the life of one of the twins even if it meant the other twin would be killed as a result.

Facts of the case
One of the twins, M, had serious brain defects, lack of proper lung tissue and did not have a working heart. Hence, M was only kept alive from the blood supply of J who had a proper functioning body system. The parents challenged the notion that it was lawful to separate the twins to save the life of J at the expense of M even though without the operation both twins would have died.

What the judge(s) said
The judges held that whilst they will respect the parents' wishes as much as they can, the courts had to decide on this matter in accordance with the ultimate welfare of the children. The operation was in the best interests of J. J would have the opportunity to lead a normal healthy life following the operation whereas M was going to die either way with or without the operation. Even though M will be killed as a result, this would not result in murder as the defence of necessity is available to the doctors. The court held that it was needed to 'avoid inevitable and irreparable evil'. It was 'no more than was reasonably necessary for the purpose to be achieved'. They decided that 'the evil to be inflicted was not disproportionate to the evil avoided'.

Why is this case important?
This case provides protection for medical practitioners who decide to perform a life-saving operation, especially on children when the parents object to the operation. Ultimately, the courts will consider the welfare of the child. As much as the parents' wishes should be respected, if the child's life is in danger the court has the power to give permission for the medical practitioners to go ahead with the operation.

The current state of the law
The child's welfare is paramount as reiterated by this case. This case tells us that medical practitioners are protected by the defence of necessity. However, they must first fulfil the test. This is a very narrow defence. It must be shown that this is necessary in order to give one twin the chance of living a healthy, fulfilling life when the other twin has had no chance to survive in the first place.

10 COMMON DEBATES/THEMES

In order to prepare for the CLT, it is useful to think about what are the sort of common legal themes and debates that are likely to come up.

Besides reading legal news frequently, you should also ideally drill down into some specific topics that you are passionate about and do thorough research on them in order to form an opinion about a divisive area of law.

If you are feeling clueless at this stage and have no idea how to go about doing your research, you should follow these tips:

- Start by reading introductory law books to get a good overall understanding. I recommend "What About Law" by Janet O'Sullivan, Graham Virgo and Catherine Barnard.
- Once you are familiar with what the word 'law' means, you should go on to focus on specific topics that might have piqued your interest.
- Go deeper into your research by googling for relevant news articles, commentaries and insights on a specific legal topic.
- If you are feeling confident, have a go at reading certain extracts of legal judgments relevant to your topic so you have an idea how legal language should be like. HE+ provides very good resources.
- Sometimes it is better for you to engage in a discussion and argument with your friends and your teachers on certain topics, as you might gain fresh ideas.
- Test out your arguments and understanding by writing practice questions and let someone else read them to see whether your writing is clear and coherent.

EUTHANASIA & MERCY KILLING

This is a highly controversial area of law and it is an area of law where it is almost impossible for everyone to come into a consensus regarding what is right and what is wrong.

Both sides of the argument can be very compelling. The argument *for* euthanasia and mercy killing is that one should not have to continue suffering in life if, for example, one is inflicted with a debilitating disease and cannot enjoy a fulfilling life. In such situations, as a human being, it is argued that we should be given the freedom to decide whether we want to continue living in illness or whether we want to end our suffering and end our lives.

The famous case of *Nicklinson* demonstrates how this argument can be very convincing; patients can be in such immense pain. As a result, this causes their family members to be severely affected. As euthanasia and mercy killing are illegal in this country, there are also many situations where people might just travel to another country where it is legal and end their lives there. This is not an available option for some patients as they might not be able travel or might not have the means to do so.

However, the counter-argument can be very convincing as well – a human life is sacred and we should not make it so easy for one to end a life without very strong safeguards. Sometimes family members might have a strong influence and persuasion on the patient to end their life – for example the patient might feel guilty for being a financial and emotional burden on his or her family members. In such situations, it would not be ideal if the law allowed for a situation where family members can pressurise a patient to end his or her life as this would undermine the sanctity of human life and the right to live.

This debate is ongoing and if this is an area that interests you, you should do some research on why certain countries allow euthanasia and mercy killing. Think about the legal issues involved – it is an offence to assist someone to die, will mercy killing be an adequate defence for such an offence?

It is important for such debates to think about both sides of the argument which has been laid down for you here in this case. It is crucial to remember that you will **not** be penalised for raising an argument that might be against the examiner's personal beliefs. Examiners mark essays neutrally and are not allowed to mark an essay based on their political beliefs or personal convictions.

In fact, sometimes a controversial essay can score extremely high marks if a student backs it up well and provides a very compelling argument with good examples. For some questions, the answer may be more 'obvious' and tend to result in most essays being rather similar and 'safe'. This makes it hard to stand out. However, do note that you should not write a controversial essay just for the sake of it. This might backfire if you fail to back it up convincingly.

PRISON

This is another divisive topic that has been regularly featured in the media. Prisons are perhaps considered quintessential in the English criminal justice system. Many people see it as a huge deterrence in committing a crime because of the fear of being incarcerated. However, English prisons are well-known to have less-than-adequate conditions and the issue of overcrowding gets exacerbated when harsher sentences are introduced as there is a lack of adequate prison facilities to accommodate the ever-increasing number of prisoners.

In contrast with English prisons, the Scandinavian system is well-known for providing very human conditions and prisons are often well-equipped. Even though it may seem counter-intuitive for prisons to provide good living conditions for prisoners, statistics have shown that re-offending rates in Scandinavian countries are extremely low. This raises the question of whether having harsh prison conditions truly result in an effective deterrence of crime.

There is also the issue of whether prison is suitable for everyone. For example, is prison a suitable solution for child offenders, female offenders, elderly offenders or disabled offenders? If not, what are the alternatives that might be available?

Due to budget cuts and an increasing pressure on the government to manage its spending on public resources, less is available for building prisons. Prisons are notoriously expensive to run due to the high security needed and the staff and facilities that need to be in place. As a result of this, the government has implemented privatisation of prisons in order to alleviate the burden of the public purse. This created several problems. Private sectors operate differently from the public sector – they focus on profit rather than welfare. It raises questions about the safety and welfare of prisoners, whether security is adequate, and whether there is an incentive for private sector operators to provide good prison services.

This is an area of law/criminology where there are numerous articles (e.g. on The Guardian) commenting on the failing prison system and the flaws and cracks in the system. These articles argue that this results in a toxic environment. This is a good area of law to think about the intersection between legal issues (e.g. criminal law and sentencing policies) as well as sociological issues (how do prisons work in deterring crime and are there other ways of preventing crime?).

There are also several documentaries available online about the prison system in England and in other countries which you can watch that will provide you with great insight and challenge your views about whether the prison system is effective as it is. There is also an interesting contrast between the Scottish criminal system versus the English criminal system.

INTERPRETATION AND IMPLICATION OF TERMS IN CONTRACTS

When we think of contracts, we usually think about what is written down and how we derive our rights and obligations from the written terms. However, there are situations when it might be appropriate to interpret the written terms in a certain way. For example, the contract may too vague. It may not be clear what are the rights and obligations that flow from the contract.

We do come across contracts more often than you might think. Think about the last time you read a contract. It might have been the terms and conditions when we download an application, or it might have been a tenancy agreement you might have signed. Certain contracts are rather straight forward so it will be clear what the rights and obligations are. An example is a simple rental agreement that will probably follow a certain standard template. For such contracts the idea of interpretation and implication of terms in a contract will not come into play.

On the other hand, not all contracts may be created under standard conditions, or not all parties are sophisticated enough to create contracts that are clear and precise. Many contracts are badly drafted; some clauses do not explicitly state what are the rights or they may be contradictory. In such situations there has been immense academic debate over to what extent judges should interpret or implicate terms into a contract in order to make it workable.

There are many ways one can go about interpreting the terms of a contract. For example, we can adopt a literal interpretation: we derive the obligations from the natural meaning of the words used in the clauses. However, such a literal interpretation will usually result in a reading of the contract that was clearly not intended by the parties. Hence, a purposive interpretation might be more appropriate.

There are many different legal tests that have been adopted by the judges in order to interpret a contract to give effect to the common intention of the parties behind the contract. For example, there is the 'business efficacy' test. Here, the judges will read the contract in a way that will make the contract work in a professional or commercial context. Judges may also have regard to the customs behind a certain contract. For example, if the contract is a simple supply agreement the judges may look at what supply agreements normally contain and interpret accordingly, unless there is strong evidence to the contrary.

Implication of terms is different from interpretation. Implication means that the judges are reading terms that were not written into the contract in the first place. This contrasts with interpreting the written terms of the contract which are already there. This might be appropriate if the parties forgot to include a clause in the contract and without the relevant clause the contract would be unworkable. Strong evidence will be needed to show that the parties intended the clause to be included, for example from their oral conversations or prior meetings that might indicate such a shared intention.

This is a very practical area of law that affects both large businesses and individual consumers. It is perhaps very different from the debates mentioned earlier as this reflects a more black-letter area of law that has been subject to a lot of academic debate. It might be harder to find relevant news articles on this topic as such practical issues may receive less media attention as they are less sensational. However, if you are interested in this area, it will be good to research on this area by looking at what sort of contracts might require different forms of interpretation, the anatomy of a contract, and why do you think contracts are quintessential in the modern commercial world.

ADVERSE POSSESSION

This is an interesting area of land law that introduces a human right issue as well. The idea of a home usually has a special connotation and people attach certain sentimental and emotional value to their home and their right to enjoy a family life.

Property rights are important as land is a finite resource – there is only so much land available to build houses on. It is not uncommon for most people to have most of their assets in the form of a property. Houses are also valuable assets for banks. Banks regularly give out mortgages in order to help homeowners purchase property, and banks stand to benefit from the interest rate that these loans generate.

Adverse possession is the concept of a 'squatter' (someone that has no legal right to the land) potentially acquiring rights to live in the property if he or she has done so for a certain period. The original owner also cannot have objected to it. This is more common in abandoned properties in secluded areas. For example, a certain farmland might have been abandoned for years and a family might have been living in an abandoned property situated on the farmland for 12 years without anyone evicting them. The family might acquire rights to continue living on the property and enjoying their family life under the doctrine of adverse possession. This doctrine helps to prevent land from being wasted and unused. It also protects the human rights of squatters who might have established a family life in a property.

However, with the introduction of the land registry, it has become significantly harder for an adverse possession claim to succeed. All land is now subject to compulsory registration. Registration in the land registry provides conclusive evidence of the legal owner of a land. Hence, a squatter who wishes to acquire a right to continue living on a particular property must apply to the land registry to register an overriding interest if the property is registered. However, doing this will tip off the original legal owner whose name is registered on the property. This gives legal owner the opportunity to refuse the application.

Again, this is a rather practical area of law that affects both homeowners as well as large commercial entities with significant real estate portfolio. However, as this is a rather controversial concept that attracts a lot of interest, there are some instances where it might come out in the news. There is a good explanation of the concept and links to news stories on HE+.

If you find this topic interesting, you should perhaps read up on the land registry. You could also read up about squatter's rights and what are the arguments for and against making it harder for squatters to acquire rights to live in a property.

Once again, both sides of the arguments can be convincing. It might seem important to protect legal owners from having their properties invaded by unknown squatters who did not pay for the property. However, on the other hand, land is a finite resource. If such properties remain unused and abandoned, and a squatter has established a long family life in the property, should the squatter be entitled to some rights in the property?

SEPARATION OF POWERS AND BREXIT

This is a topic that has received a lot of media attention lately because of the discussions surrounding Brexit.

Our constitutional system is centred around the separation of powers between the legislative, executive and judiciary. The idea behind the need for a separation of powers is to prevent an abuse of power as well as to ensure that the separate entities can specialise in one area and gain the necessary expertise.

Brexit raised the issue of separation of powers as it was argued that the government (the executive), did not have the necessary powers to trigger Article 50. Article 50 was needed in order to initiate the process of leaving the EU. It was argued that since Parliament was the one that granted EU law supreme status, Parliament should be the one who gets to say whether we wished to end this relationship between domestic law and EU law. For more details, you can refer to the section where the Supreme Court case brought by Gina Miller is discussed.

Separation of powers does not necessarily mean one entity will not have any powers to perform a role that is left to another entity – for example, judges have certain limited law-making powers, and the executive may have certain limited judiciary powers.

This is an area of law that has produced several commentaries, news articles as well as the Supreme Court judgment itself that has been reported on multiple times. Hence, there is a wealth of resources for you to explore.

Do take note that this issue can be very heavily politicised, hence you must be mindful of only focusing on the **legal** issues behind such a political issue. For example, why is the doctrine of separation of powers so important, why are the three entities tasked to perform their separate tasks accordingly, how do the three entities work together to create the legal system of England and Wales, and why did Brexit create so much furore over such constitutional issues?

This is a highly popular area of law that students like to discuss and mention in their personal statements and in the interviews. The good thing is that this is a very topical issue and very relevant with a lot of legal issues to discuss. The bad thing is that students may struggle to disassociate from the heavy political undertones. This results in writing an essay to veers too much towards being political and may lead to a bad mark.

In order to stand out in writing about such a topic, make sure you do in-depth research and find out what the legal issues behind separation of powers are and why did Brexit create so much interest in this topic. Ideally you should focus on commentaries from legal academics instead of politicians. Politicians tend to focus more on sensational facts to appeal to the public as opposed to providing a precise legal analysis.

ALTERNATIVE FAMILY STRUCTURES

This topic has gained increasing traction as society becomes more modern. People are becoming more liberal in general and accepting of different forms of family structures and relationships.

Family law in England and Wales has gradually developed to accept different forms of relationship, with the implementation of civil partnerships for same-sex partners and subsequently legalising same-sex marriage.

Laws are also put in place to ensure that sperm donors do not acquire parenthood rights over a child in order to protect the legal parents from any potential disruption of their family unit. Furthermore, adoption laws also ensure that parents of an adopted child have their parenthood rights protected.

Cohabitation is a contentious issue and there have been plenty of arguments calling for greater protection of cohabitants. This is in response to the rise in cohabitation arrangements as younger couples prefer cohabitation over marriage. Many couples have raised the idea that they do not agree with the religious notion behind marriage, or they shun the societal expectations behind marriage such as the female almost always being the weaker party in a marriage.

Arguments for and against providing greater protection for cohabitants can be convincing. Whilst it is arguable that cohabitants should be provided adequate legal protection, detractors argue that this waters down the notion of a marriage. Those in support argue that cohabitants can enjoyed a stable and loving relationship which is in fact not much different from what a married couple enjoys.

For many traditionalists, they feel that marriage still represents the 'gold standard' of a relationship and entering a marriage signifies a life-long commitment and has a strong symbolic notion. These people argue that by recognising cohabitation and providing stronger legal protection for cohabitants, this undermines the idea of marriage and consequently weakens the already diminishing idea behind marriage being the end-goal of a relationship.

There are also issues of who can be considered a 'parent' of a child, especially with same-sex couples who wish to have children. Many of them may use various methods to have children. For example, they may use a surrogate mother, a sperm donor, adoption or other possible methods to have a child, and the issue of parenthood gets complicated accordingly.

Surrogacy also creates a lot of ethical and legal issues: to what extent should we allow surrogacy agreements to take place, how do we provide adequate protection for a surrogate mother in entering such an arrangement, and does surrogacy provide a good way of helping couples in having a child if they otherwise could not have due to fertility issues?

This is a hot topic in law and there are plenty of news articles, commentaries and real-life examples that can be drawn if you are interested in this topic. There are many ethical issues to ponder over, as well as human rights issues and how the notion of a 'family' or a 'relationship' has changed drastically over the years.

JURY SYSTEM

This is an interesting topic partly because the jury system receives a lot of attention in our criminal justice system. This is also an area of law that is very familiar with most laypeople, whether be it people who have served jury duty before or just from watching legal dramas.

The idea behind a jury system is simple – the public should get a say in our criminal justice system. People argue that judges are too detached from the public therefore we have the jury system to represent the public view. The jury is there to decide the case based on the facts presented, the law is left to the judge and the judge directs the jury to consider the facts and presents to the jury what the law is.

Not all jurisdictions have a jury system. In England and Wales, the jury system was abolished for civil claims. There are obvious pros and cons behind a jury system and it has been debated whether a jury system serves a benefit or whether it leads to unsafe convictions.

The benefit of a jury system is that it helps to uphold faith in the judicial system, such that the public knows that they have a say in criminal cases. This will help dispel any connotations that judges might be biased or corrupted and have absolute power to convict defendants and send them to jail.

The downside of a jury system is the potential flaws behind asking laypeople to decide a case based on the facts. The risk of jury tampering is a serious one, and perhaps something that has been portrayed in legal dramas several times due to its sensational nature. There is also the risk of jury bias, for example certain jurors may have hidden prejudices or perceptions towards people of a certain race, religion or gender.

In this age of social media, there has also been an added risk of inappropriate communication of the case and juries receiving inappropriate information about the case. For example, think about the problems behind a juror 'live-tweeting' about a case during deliberations or even during the trial itself.

There is also an issue of who should serve in the jury – individuals with a potential conflict of interest should not serve in the jury – for example if the juror knows the defendant, or is a member of the legal profession and has worked on a similar case before and thus has a vested interest.

Jury deliberations can also be problematic. For example, as a unanimous decision is needed from a jury before a defendant can be convicted, you get prolonged deliberations when a unanimous decision cannot be reached. Some jurors may be pressurised into changing their votes by more aggressive members of the jury, or they may simply get tired and just want to get out of the deliberation room sooner. There have also been reported cases of inappropriate ways of deciding on a case, such as a jury using a Ouija board to decide on a case!

This is a good topic to do some research on as it touches on procedural issues behind criminal law and provides some good insight in the criminal justice system.

NATURAL LAW VS. POSITIVE LAW

This is a jurisprudential question (the philosophy of law) that has created hundreds of years of debate. This is interesting if you find the philosophy of law thought-provoking and wonder what the word 'law' really means. The main proponent of positive law is usually attributable to Hart, who writes extensively about positive law in his book *The Concept of Law*. However, he does seek to distance himself from what he calls the 'hard positivists', namely Raz and Austin.

Hart believes that we benefit from separating what the law is from what the law should be. He believed this aided clarity in thought and helped us fully understand what law really is. The opponents of Hart range from Dworkin to Fuller to Finnis, which shows how influential and controversial Hart was.

The natural law position does not treat law as 'whatever Parliament says law is'. Rather, natural law indicates that there are certain laws that are so fundamental to human life that they exist regardless of whether Parliament has enacted them as laws or not. For example, natural lawyers might argue that certain actions such as killing someone without a defence will never be lawful even if the law makes it lawful as such.

This debate produces interesting questions in real life beyond the theoretical and abstract. For example, under the Nazi regime it was the 'law' that the soldiers could kill Jewish people just because they were Jewish. Positive lawyers say that since that was the 'law' implemented by the regime. We cannot ignore the fact that what the soldiers were doing were lawful at that time. We would have to accept the fact that we would be retrospectively repealing the law if we were to convict the soldiers later for war crime.

However, natural lawyers oppose this conclusion. They believe that laws that are so evil and against the fundamental rights of human beings can never be lawful and that the laws implemented by the evil Nazi regime were never laws to begin with. Hence, they indicate that the soldiers were always acting unlawfully even if they were acting under orders.

Jurisprudence is a perfect example of an area of law where you can basically debate endlessly about which position is right and which position is wrong without ever coming into a consensus. This is a good area for you to do some research on. It basically encapsulates every other area of law and provides a good philosophical foundation of why we call some laws 'law' and what constitutes a valid law.

PURE ECONOMIC LOSS

This is an area of tort that has been constantly developing and has been a crucial area in commercial settings as businesses are potentially liable for huge amounts of loss that are purely economic loss.

Pure economic loss can be contrasted with physical damage such as being injured while at work, or psychological damage such as suffering trauma as a result of witnessing an accident. For example, one might not be able to work following an accident, and the period of loss of wages will count as pure economic loss.

Pure economic loss can be hard to define because it can potentially be unlimited and wide-ranging. If an accident causes a victim to be permanently paralysed for example, they can potentially claim for a loss of earnings for the whole of their potential career.

The problem with assessing such loss is that it can be very speculative in nature – how long was the victim going to work for, what kind of job was he going to get, how much was he going to be paid, and would he be promoted or get a pay raise?

There is also the issue of 'intervening events', such as if the victim contracts a disease unrelated to the accident later on – will this be an event that causes the victim to lose his ability to work and hence relieve the original defendant of liability for compensation?

Pure economic loss is given a rather different treatment in the US, with astronomical claims being awarded. There was an infamous McDonald's incident where millions of dollars were awarded to a claimant who got scalded as a result of McDonald's serving her hot coffee.

The US provides a good case study for pure economic loss because of their more liberal attitude towards awarding damages for pure economic loss. This has resulted in a highly litigious attitude in the US where lawsuits are brought frequently in the hopes of receiving large awards of compensation. This contrasts with the UK where judges are more conservative in awarding damages for pure economic loss and there are more barriers in place to ensure that such claims are not awarded too frivolously.

The issue with awarding compensation for pure economic loss too easily is that it 'opens the floodgates' for litigation. Judges in the UK are afraid that this might result in many frivolous claims being brought.

This is an important area of tort law that has a lot of interesting discussion. It raises commercial issues as well as the economic issues. Students who have an interest in private law and the commercial issues behind such damages should research more on this area and form an opinion about whether the US or the UK system treats pure economic loss more ideally.

VICARIOUS LIABILITY

Vicarious liability means the liability of an employer for the actions of an employee or worker – for example can an employer be liable for the harm done to someone as a result of an employee's actions?

This area of law has perhaps gained some prominence following the Grenfell incident. The issue here was whether the company who failed to provide cladding that was fireproof should be held liable for the deaths of the victims. This topic is also important in the context of workplace bullying. For example, there have been reported cases of employees suffering from depression or trauma as a result of workplace bullying or discrimination. Should an employer be liable for the acts of such employees?

Companies, especially large corporations, usually have extensive human resources practices in place to ensure that such workplace bullying or discrimination do not take place. For example, there will be strict company guidelines that prohibit such behaviour, and there will be information and training sessions to ensure that staff know about the prohibition behind workplace harassment and bullying.

Vicarious liability may also provide a good means of enforcing a claim. For example, a victim may prefer suing the company over the individual who perpetuated the action because the company has 'deeper pockets'. Suing an individual might not result in much compensation as the individual will not be able to afford it but companies are usually more able to pay out large compensations.

There is also a related employment law issue of who can be constituted as an employee or worker. This has received tremendous media attention following the Uber judgments and the rise of the gig economy. For example, if an Uber driver is accused of sexual harassment, to what extent should Uber as a company be liable? This is an issue because Uber claims that all its drivers are 'self-employed'. In 2021, the Supreme Court ruled that Uber drivers are workers and not self-employed. Academics think that this ruling has wider implications for a lot of other gig economy workers like private hire drivers, couriers and delivery drivers.

Even though companies may describe their employees or workers as 'self-employed', the courts will be less sympathetic to the employers if the facts indicate that the workers are under the control of the employer or are integrated into their system. This is an area of law that permeates other law subjects besides tort such as employment law and contract law. It provides good fodder for discussion regarding to what extent employers should be liable for the actions of an employee. A good starting point would be to perhaps read up about the gig economy and the Uber fiasco that has been heavily reported in the news, followed by forming an opinion regarding how much liability should be attributable to an employer and what are the pros and cons of doing so.

HOW TO WRITE YOUR ESSAY

As mentioned in the assessment criteria provided by the Faculty of Law, not only is the content of your essay important, you will have to ensure that the structure is clear and easy to follow, your arguments are made in a succinct and coherent manner, and you have truly engaged with the question and shown critical analysis.

You have a total of one hour to write your essay, so make sure you utilise this time wisely and properly set out your structure beforehand to ensure that you keep on track. Planning is essential to ensure that you do not go off on a tangent or forget to address the question directly. A common mistake is that students tend to get carried away as they are writing an essay and forget to always refer to what the question is asking. An essay may be brilliantly written but if it does not answer the exact question, it is going to be a failing mark. This is how you should allocate your time:

First 5 minutes	• Read carefully over the questions and choose your question wisely - only pick something that you are familiar and confident with. Make sure you have fully understood what the question is asking.
Next 10 minutes	• Plan out your essay by thinking about your structure; • Set out your main arguments on a rough paper in point form so you do not forget them as you go along.
Next 35-40 minutes	• Write the essay and make sure you always answer the question being asked and do not get carried away; • Make sure at all times what you are writing is clear, coherent and provides a good analysis of the question.
Last 5-10 minutes	• Give yourself ample time to check through your answer to ensure that there are no grammatical and spelling mistakes; • Giving yourself ample time to finish will also ensure that you do not hand in a rushed essay with no conclusion.

STRUCTURING YOUR ESSAY

The structure of an essay can be broken down into three key elements – the introduction, the main body and the conclusion.

The main body is further split into 2-4 paragraphs that provide different key points to bolster your main argument, as well as addressing the relevant counter-arguments and showing why the counter-arguments fail to undermine your main argument.

You should always check on the Law Faculty website to see if the format and type of questions has changed as they do change them relatively frequently. There are also sample tests on the website for you to look at and practice. Previously, there were several different types of questions that they could ask you. However, they have now changed it and they only set discursive essay-type questions.

A discursive essay question will be one that usually challenges you to think about an area of law. For example, 'Some forms of conduct that would normally constitute a criminal offence will not constitute such an offence if the person affected by the conduct has consented to it. (a) Do you agree that this is a sensible position for the law to have adopted? (Sample 2)'. They could also ask questions that have a philosophical or controversial element such as 'Do we owe greater moral duties to our family and friends than we owe to all other people in the world? Why, or why not? (Sample 3).

You can adopt the same straightforward structure for both types. In such essay questions, it will be advisable to set out your main argument in the introduction early on to not leave the examiner 'guessing' throughout the essay what you are trying to argue.

There are usually no right and wrong answers. In fact, sometimes candidates stand out and do exceptionally well by putting forward a difficult and controversial argument. This is only if they go on to explain it well and provide a highly convincing defence against the counterarguments that can be raised. You should avoid being overly one-sided and only raise points that are supportive of your main argument in the main body. A good essay should address and acknowledge the relevant counter-arguments that can be raised, and then go on to show how these counter-arguments are weaker than the main argument being put forward.

The structure of an essay can be shown as follows:

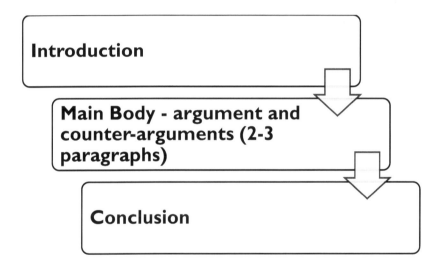

THE EXAM APPROACH

Most problems are caused by a lack of planning and poor essay selection. Students typically just want to get writing as they are worried about finishing on time. Always resist the temptation of writing your essay straightaway without putting in thought as to how to structure your essay and to set out your arguments clearly and succinctly. A well-structured, clear and coherent essay will always be better than a longer, but more muddled essay which is hard for an examiner to follow.

Here is a summary of a good exam approach:

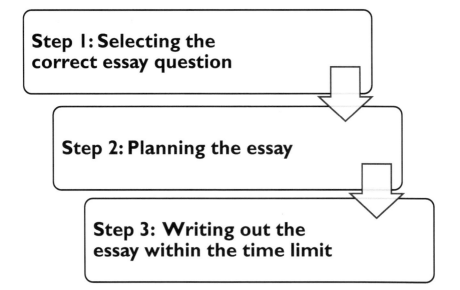

Step 1: Selecting the correct essay question

Step 2: Planning the essay

Step 3: Writing out the essay within the time limit

STEP 1: SELECTING AN ESSAY QUESTION

You will be given a choice of 3 essays to choose from and crucially, you will have no idea of what it could be beforehand. Selecting your essay is crucial - make sure you're comfortable with the topic and ensure you have read and understood the actual question. A fatal mistake you can make is to write an entire essay without once answering the exact question asked. You should always ensure that you refer to the question in your answer and fully understand a question before you attempt it. If are unsure what the question is really asking, it is usually a clear sign that you should not choose that question.

Take your time to read all the questions and decide which one you understand the most and will be most confident in. Although one essay question might originally seem easy, if you haven't thought through it, you might quickly find yourself running out of ideas. Likewise, a seemingly difficult essay might offer you a good opportunity to make interesting points. If you perform well in a difficult essay as opposed to writing an average essay for an easier question, it also usually reflects well on you. Examiners tend to give credit for students who attempt questions that are more challenging and successfully write a strong essay for it. However, you should not risk doing this if you do not understand the question fully – in that case you should stick to topics that you are comfortable with.

Use this time to carefully select which question you will answer by gauging how accessible and comfortable you are with it given your background knowledge.

It's surprisingly easy to misinterpret a question and change it into something similar, but with a different meaning. Thus, you may end up answering a question you wished had come up rather than the actual question that was set. Once you've decided which question you're going to do, read it very carefully a few times to make sure you fully understand it. Answer all aspects of the question. Keep reading it as you answer to ensure you stay on track!

STEP 2: PLANNING

The importance of planning

Students are often tempted to write an essay the minute you spot a question that you are familiar with. However, you should always take some time initially to create a rough plan for your essay. This is crucial for setting out a good structure that provides a clear answer that is easy to read. It will also prevent you from getting carried away writing that you forget what main points you are going to make or fail to answer the question whilst writing the essay. Remember, here are some things that the examiners look out for in a good CLT essay:

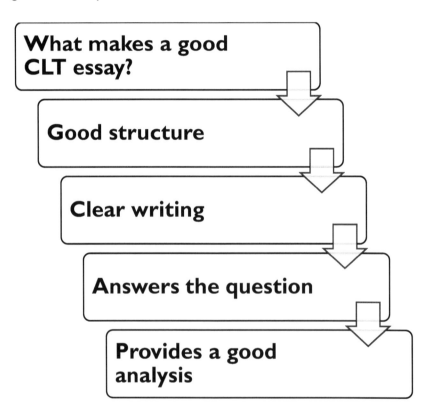

What makes a good CLT essay?

Good structure

Clear writing

Answers the question

Provides a good analysis

On the flip side of the coin, you should not take too much time planning your essay and leave yourself short of time when you are writing out your essay! As a rough guide, you should spend no more than **10 minutes** planning an essay. The CLT is time pressured as you only get an hour to write your essay. This includes your reading time hence you need to give yourself some allowance of time in reading the questions, selecting a question and planning for it accordingly.

What does planning entail?

Planning differs from every individual, but in general make sure you think about what the main points you will be raising and number them accordingly. This is to ensure that you have thought about the possible counter-arguments that can be made against your essay and how you are going to tackle them. This also helps you write an effective introduction. A good essay should have at least 2-3 main points which translates into 2-3 main body paragraphs.

Always keep in mind the general structure of an essay and plan accordingly:

Introduction : How am I answering the question and what points will I make?

Main body: How many points will I be making and how am I going to address my counter-arguments/have I identified all the issues mentioned in the question?

Conclusion: How can I effectively sum up what my argument is or what my final conclusion is having analysed all the issues raised?

STEP 3: WRITING

Introduction

The introduction should explain your position and define any key terms. Here, you should say what you're going to say and suggest (either affirmatively or tentatively) a response or answer to the question. It is always a good idea to set out clearly what your thesis is going to be. For example, do you agree or disagree with the statement and your reasons for agreeing or disagreeing. This will tell the examiner straightaway what your opinion is instead of leaving them to guess what your point is – it does not reflect well on you when the examiners are unable to grasp what you are trying to argue!

It is important not to spend too long on an introduction as that would use up too much time. This time could be better spent on other parts of the essay. However, bear in mind that a good, clear and succinct introduction sets a very good impression for an examiner and might pull up your marks.

In summary, this is what you should include in your introduction:

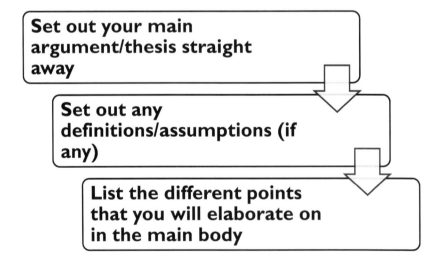

Set out your main argument/thesis straight away

Set out any definitions/assumptions (if any)

List the different points that you will elaborate on in the main body

MAIN BODY

The importance of plain, simple English

The purpose of your essay is to show how you can provide good analysis of the question asked, raise relevant examples, identify as many issues as possible and tackle any possible counterarguments. Using superfluous and flamboyant language and vocabulary will not get you far – you will have to adopt a precise, academic-style of writing for the CLT.

Tone and style

Unlike other essay-based subjects that you might have done, you should not be adopting an aggressive or emotional style of writing for the CLT. You should be adopting a neutral tone and seek to provide a good analysis of the question in a logical manner. Avoid adopting a style that reads more like a novel or a personal blog as opposed to an academic piece of writing. If you are in doubt, you should read more newspaper articles from a credible source (e.g. Financial Times, The Economist) in order to have a feel of what a precise style of writing should be.

Structure

It is common for students to start the first paragraph of their main body by addressing the counter-argument first, so they can focus on developing the points in favour of their main argument in the subsequent body paragraphs. Another good approach is to start off with your strongest and main points first. This is good to ensure that at the very least, your main points are down on the page for the examiner to read. Whichever style you adopt, make sure you do not run out of time and fail to include the points that are most important for you to answer the question well.

Headings

Headings are optional, but highly recommended as they can be useful in providing a signpost for the examiner to understand the different arguments you are raising. Headings do not need to be complicated and should summarise in two to three words what the point of the paragraph(s) are.

Legalistic terms

Since no prior legal knowledge is expected of students taking the CLT, you do not have to worry about trying to incorporate precise legal terms in your essay (especially Latin terms!). You may use the legal terms used in the CLT question itself. You are also not expected to construct any technical arguments. Any arguments you construct in relation to the CLT question which reference legal terms can come from more general concepts like the welfare principle, utilitarianism or paternalism. Whilst it is good if you are aware of the terms and how they are used precisely, avoid using them if you are unsure about their exact meaning as this might backfire, especially if you use a complex legal term wrongly and skew the whole meaning of your essay.

Remember these few points in order to write out a good main body, which forms the bulk of your essay:

Structure
- Make sure your paragraphs or sentences are not too long;
- Headings are useful to signal what your different arguments are.

Style &Tone
- Avoid an overly casual tone;
- Use precise, clear English.

Content
- Always answer the question and raise relevant examples when appropriate;
- Make sure you have elaborated sufficiently o each of your point to support your argument.

CONCLUSION

Finally, this is where you can catch your breath and pat yourself on the back for a job well done! However, many students tend to neglect the conclusion, either because they run out of time or they simply do not know what to include. A good conclusion provides a good overall impression of your essay on the examiner and can go a long way in helping you achieve a good mark.

Summary of your argument

You will want to provide a good summary of your argument in order to reiterate what your main argument is and how you arrived at the conclusion. For a problem question, you will want to state your overall legal advice or solution based on the fact pattern provided.

Short and sweet

Your conclusion should only be a short, final concluding paragraph. Do not use this paragraph to introduce new ideas – any new points should be included in the main paragraph! Also avoid repeating what you have stated in the introduction, this is a good opportunity for you to write a short, punchy conclusion that leaves an impression on the examiner and helps drive home the main argument you are trying to make.

EXAMPLE ESSAY TITLES

1. Should euthanasia be legalised? Why or why not?
2. Should judges be elected?
3. The jury system should be abolished. Discuss.
4. Should squatters in a property ever get a right to continue living in the property?
5. Do you think cohabitants should enjoy the same legal rights as married couples?
6. In English law companies are considered to have their own legal personality which means that they can make contracts, must pay taxes, can sue and be sued. Do you think companies should be capable of being convicted of crimes? If so, in what circumstances do you think companies should be convicted?
7. Discuss whether the sentence of a convicted individual should be reduced in the following situations:
   a. Chris claims that he only stole from a shop because he had to provide for his sick son;
   b. Dennis claims that he only exposed himself in public because he was drunk;
   c. Eloise claims that she only robbed someone because she was addicted to drugs and she has since sought help.
8. An employee suffers serious injuries after a freak accident in the workplace involving heavy machinery. How should the liability be apportioned between:
   a. The employee himself;
   b. The direct manager supervising the employee;
   c. The directors of the company.
9. Do you agree that laws are what Parliament enact as laws only?
10. What other systems of laws can you think of besides English common law and how do they differ from English common law?

11. Do you think the gig economy (e.g. Uber, Deliveroo) undermines employment rights or do you think they are a necessary response to economic changes?

12. To what extent should medical discoveries be free for all to exploit instead of being protected under intellectual property law?

13. Discuss whether the following contracts are valid and why:
    a. A contract for an uncle to give a nephew £300 on the condition that the nephew passes his exams;
    b. A contract for an escort to provide services to a client;
    c. A contract to produce 50 chocolate wrappers in exchange for a prize.

14. What are the potential legal issues behind allowing unrestricted freedom of movement of persons between the EU member states?

15. Some forms of conduct that would normally constitute a criminal offence will not constitute such an offence if the person affected by the conduct has consented to it.
    (a) Do you agree that this is a sensible position for the law to have adopted?
    and
    (b) Should consent on the part of the person affected by the conduct always have the effect of relieving the person who undertook the conduct of criminal liability? In addressing this matter, consider the following situations:
    (i) a boxing match;
    (ii) the killing of a terminally-ill person who wishes to be killed.

FULLY WORKED ESSAYS

EXAMPLE ESSAY 1

Who should not be allowed to serve on the jury and why?

Better Response:
This essay will argue that the following individuals should not be allowed to serve: (1) *individuals who are at risk of undermining the public confidence of the criminal justice system and (2)individuals who are likely to not exercise independent judgment when serving as a juror. The former includes individuals who have a conflict of interest. For example, a police officer who has worked on a similar case before might have a vested interest. The latter includes individuals who have shown that they possess a certain prejudiced viewpoint, such as being more sceptical of certain religious groups.*

It might be argued that we should ban all individuals who are connected to the criminal justice system from serving as jurors. This would include several members such as judges, magistrates, police officers, solicitors and barristers. However, we run the risk of depriving many of these individuals who might be willing and able to serve as jury members. While the concern that they will allow their own legal knowledge to influence their decision is valid, the idea of a jury system is to let the jury members assess a case based on its facts, with the judge directing the jury accordingly as to what the law is.

However, this is a broad generalisation and there are individuals connected that can exercise independent judgment. This is especially true if they are legally trained as they are expected to know the role of the jury and how they should go about deciding the case as a jury member. The only exception we should make are individuals who might have a vested interest in the case, such as a police officer who has worked on a similar case before. This is because the police officer might be tempted to decide the current case similarly. Such individuals should not be allowed to serve as a jury member on that specific case (as opposed to a general ban), in order to uphold the public's confidence in the jury system as the public expects the jury system to be independent.

There are also arguments that we should have a proportionate representation in the jury so that minority groups are well-represented. For example, we should ensure that the jury system is not just made up fully of a certain race, religion or social background. However, whilst this is a valid sentiment, this is largely unworkable as we will have to create an artificial situation where out of 12 jury members, we will have to ensure that there is one member of each minority group. The purpose of the jury system is to ensure that the public is represented in the jury system and the jury can exercise independent, value-free judgement in order to decide upon a defendant's guilt based on the facts of the case.

If the defendant is part of a minority group, it is a valid concern that the jury might not be sensitive to the defendant's background if they are comprised entirely of a different racial or religious group. However, the solution to this is to ensure that jurors are adequately informed and prepped beforehand. This ensures that they know that any judgments made in favour or against the defendant should never be based on prejudice or stereotype. If it is discovered during the initial screening process that a certain potential juror exhibits a strong tendency to have a biased opinion, then such a juror should be removed.

In conclusion, we should only disallow someone from being a juror member if there is a significant risk of conflict of interest, such as a member who has worked on a similar case before, or if there is a significant risk of a biased opinion, such as an individual who has exhibited a strong tendency to have prejudicial opinions.

Examiner's Comments:

Overall: This is a strong response – it answers the questions directly and provides an in-depth analysis of the thorny issues surrounding this topic. It shows a level of maturity and insight that goes beyond what is expected. This essay will likely score an 8 or 9 on the scale. It will stand a good chance of getting an offer.

Introduction: The introduction directly answers the question and tells the examiner immediately what the author's thesis will be. It sets out nicely what will be expanded on in the main body. It has focused on the thorny issues raised by the question instead of wasting time talking about the less controversial issues such as age and mental capacity.

Main Body: The main body shows a very high level of analysis of the two thorny issues raised by the author in the introduction. Even though there are only two main paragraphs, this is a perfect example of quality over quantity. It is better to have two main paragraphs which are analysed in detail than to have four paragraphs which are merely glossed over without showing an in-depth analysis. The author is not afraid to lay out his/her opinion in controversial issues such as the issue of proportionate representation in the jury, and they tackle the counter-arguments well in order to bolster their own argument. There is no right or wrong answer. As long as you have made a good attempt at addressing the counter-arguments and defending your own opinion, this will result in higher marks being awarded beyond the 'safe' range.

Conclusion: The conclusion once again nicely wraps up what has been argued thus far and provides a good summary to remind the examiner of the main argument being put forward in the essay.

Worse Response:

The jury has been traditionally made up of laypersons randomly selected in order to represent the public in deciding a case. Whether someone should be selected as juror or not is a subjective question and this will require us to examine all the circumstances of the case. We will have to look at factors such as someone's age, mental capacity, profession, family background, racial and religious background and sexuality.

Firstly, if someone is too young, they will not be a good fit for a jury because they will lack the necessary experience and the ability to evaluate a case with enough maturity. On the flip side, if someone is too old, this might impinge on their ability to pay close attention to their entire trial process, especially if their memory is not as good.

We also should not allow people with mental illnesses to serve in the jury as they will not have enough mental capacity to handle a trial process. Ideally, someone serving in the jury should have a sound mind, capable of exercising independent judgment.

Members of the public serving in certain sensitive or regulated professions should also be excluded from serving in the jury. For example, police officers and judges may have a conflict of interest by serving in the jury. They should be excluded to uphold the public's confidence in the jury system. Similarly, solicitors and barristers should also be excluded if they are likely to be affected by their pre-existing knowledge of the law instead of evaluating the case based on the facts and evidence presented before them.

We must also ensure that the jury accurately reflects the general public, hence there should be a diverse range of jurors from different family, religious and racial backgrounds. If all the jurors only represented one group, this might result in a strong risk of biasness and result in either an unfair outcome or the public losing confidence in the jury system. This is especially the case if the defendant happens to be from a minority group that is underrepresented.

Overall, the selection of a juror is very context-specific and we will have to look at several factors and criteria in order to decide whether someone should be part of the jury.

Examiner's Comments:

Overall: This is a valid essay, there are no major errors (e.g. not answering the question, major grammatical or spelling errors). However, it is a very 'safe' essay. It sits on the fence and does not answer the question directly, as evident from the introduction and conclusion. Hence, this will not achieve a very high mark, it will probably achieve a 5 or 6 on the scale, which means that it will not stand a very strong chance of getting an offer. It does not analyse the points raised in enough depth.

Introduction: The introduction does not explicitly answer the question, which is made up of two parts – 'who should not serve in the jury' and 'why?'. It is perfectly fine to define the jury system and explain how a juror is selected in the current system, but it is preferable for you to start your introduction by answering the question directly, so that the examiner knows straightaway what your stance is and how you are going to defend it in the subsequent paragraphs. Sitting on the fence, such as saying 'it depends on the circumstances' or 'we must look at the facts' generally indicates a very 'safe' essay that does not answer the question directly. It will result in a 'safe' mark, meaning one that will not go beyond a 6.

Main Body: Overall, the points made in the main body are valid but rather superficial. For example, age and mental capacity and rather obvious factors. It is better for you to start off your main body by tackling the more controversial issues that require more explanation, such as the background of a potential juror and members of certain professions in this case. This also ensures that if you run out of time, you can skip the less controversial issues and focus your time on the topics that require more discussion. There is a lack of a more in-depth analysis of the controversial issues in this essay, and it is perhaps rather one-sided. You should always attempt at addressing the counter-arguments to strengthen your own argument and make it as fool-proof as possible.

Conclusion: Again, the conclusion suffers from the same problem as the introduction – it does not answer the question. A conclusion should be a good summary of your arguments thus far and this is a good point to remind the examiner again of your thesis. Here, the candidate is simply repeating that selecting a juror is 'context-specific'. This will not add any value to your essay.

EXAMPLE ESSAY 2

Laws should always be created by Parliament and no one else. To what extent do you agree?

Better response:

This essay will disagree with the statement. While Parliament should solely be responsible for law-making due to the fundamental principle of separation of powers in terms of creating statutory law, there are other areas of law-making that should be given to the judiciary and executive.

For example, judges should have the power to exercise their discretion in areas where Parliament thinks judges are better placed to exercise their judgment. This includes deciding the sentence of a defendant or determining the mental element of certain offences such as fraud which requires a lot of subjective judgment. The executive should be given limited powers for certain areas that will aid them in running the government, such as being given powers to legislate in administrative areas such as the administration of cities. This can be seen from the usage of statutory instruments.

Only parliament should be responsible.

The main reason why it is true that Parliament should be solely responsible for law-making in terms of creating statutory law is because Parliament, as the legislative body, is democratically elected and represents the will of the population. Hence, under the idea of democratic legitimacy, Parliament is the only body who can create laws that create restrictions on the general public as they are merely reflecting the will of the democracy. If another body were to create statutory law, such as the judiciary or the executive, this will create the risk of unelected bodies creating laws that affect the freedom and rights of the general public and go against the fundamental idea of democratic legitimacy.

The judiciary

However, Parliament cannot envisage every single situation that will be governed by law and the flexibility and adaptiveness of our common law system makes it necessary for our judges to have certain limited law-making powers. For example, the idea of stare decisis (i.e. judgments by higher courts being binding and have precedential value) allows judges to have a certain law-making power in a way as they can decide cases that become binding authority. This is especially useful for certain context-specific cases that Parliament will not be able to envisage at the time of writing the statute. This power wielded by judges is limited as it is always up to Parliament to re-write the statute and override the decided case if they are unhappy with the judgment and think it goes against their intention. Hence, judges possess a powerful, albeit limited law-making power under the common law system and can decide on cases that require their discretion, including sentencing and deciding on the level of intention of a defendant.

The executive

The executive, being the body in charge of running the country as the government, are mainly enforcing the laws that have been enacted by Parliament and should technically not be allowed to create laws due to conflict of interest. However, in the interest of ensuring the smooth-running of the country, certain administrative tasks should be delegated to the executive so they can create rules that are binding and do not have to go through the onerous, lengthy process of parliamentary law-making. For example, certain administrative functions such as planning laws and town council regulations should be left to the executive as they are more familiar with the requirements and can create binding rules accordingly such as using statutory instruments. Hence, they are provided with limited powers under a specific domain to create laws.

In conclusion, the main power of law-making should still be solely vested with Parliament, with the exception of limited powers being conferred on the judiciary and executive so as to allow them to perform their functions more effectively without impinging on the legislative domain of the legislative.

Examiner's Comments:

Overall: This essay handles the question well. It gives a very thorough and nuanced analysis of why Parliament should be the only entity that creates law with important exceptions. The explanation provided shows a high level of further reading and the candidate has clearly read up a lot about constitutional law issues. This essay will likely achieve 8 and stand a very high chance of getting an offer. The essay also makes use of headings which make it easy for the examiner to follow the main points.

Introduction: The introduction answers the question directly and sets out the arguments the author will be putting forward with examples. Itis an effective introduction that allows the examiner to follow the main body with ease.

Main Body: The three paragraphs are easy to follow as the three main points have already been set out in the introduction, which shows clarity in structure. Good structure is imperative to scoring a good mark. The author also makes use of good examples based on his/her further reading. They have shown a good level of understanding of constitutional principles such as the idea of separation of powers and democratic legitimacy. The author has shown an impressive level of understanding and awareness that goes beyond what is typically expected of an applicant who has yet to read law. These factors all point towards the essay being deserving of a high mark.

Conclusion: The conclusion is short and effective, summarising the author's arguments and reinforcing the main thesis.

Worse response:
Parliament should not be the only entity that creates laws as judges are more well-suited to do so. Judges are legally trained, understand the law better and can create laws that will protect more rights and lead to greater regulation of certain crimes. Hence, judges should also be allowed to make laws.

Parliament consists of Members of Parliament (MPs), and these MPs often do not have a legal background. Furthermore, they tend to pander to popular interest, hence they only enact laws that will help them achieve more votes, such as enforcing stricter laws against immigration because the general public is getting frustrated over the presence of more foreigners. Such law-making does not benefit the country, as these politicians are self-interested and only care about being elected again in the next cycle, and result in laws that are ineffective and do not focus on the long-term benefit of the country.

We need judges to create law as they are legally trained and know how to create laws that will result in less crime and create laws that offer better protection to fundamental human rights. For example, judges constantly hear many criminal cases, and know how to tweak the law accordingly to reduce the chances of criminals flouting the law. Judges also understand human rights better than politicians and know how to create laws that allow better protection of such rights. Whereas politicians tend to have a more superficial and layperson understanding of human rights, such as not considering human rights when implementing draconian immigration laws just as a result of reacting to the general public's desire.

Hence, judges are more well-placed to decide on what laws should be created, instead of politicians who are self-interested and do not have the requisite legal knowledge.

Examiner's Comments:

Overall: This essay unfortunately shows a lack of understanding of constitutional issues and comes across as too 'layperson'. There is no mention whatsoever of the executive, and the essay is too one-sided. It fails to analyse the reason why we might insist on Parliament being the only entity capable of creating laws. There is no mention or any attempt of discussing concepts such as democratic legitimacy of the legislative, or what different roles the judiciary and executive play. This essay will not do well and will probably receive a failing mark of 4.

Introduction: The introduction does answer the question. However, it also becomes clear from the outset that the author does not have a sufficient understanding of the question and has gone completely off-track. When you are not confident that you fully understand a question or have read up enough about the issues surrounding a certain topic, it is strongly advisable for you to attempt another question.

Main Body: The author does adopt a sensible structure by talking about the two main points raised in the introduction separately. However, the analysis done shows a lack of understanding of fundamental constitutional principles. There is no attempt at all in addressing counter-arguments which unfortunately weakens the essay by making it overly one-sided.

Conclusion: The conclusion is acceptable, but for the reasons mentioned above the essay is weak and shows a lack of understanding.

EXAMPLE ESSAY 3

Should the courts allow a child to refuse a blood transfusion because he is a Jehovah's Witness, even though without the blood transfusion the child will die?

Better response:

The court should only allow a child to refuse consent to blood transfusion if the consent is genuine, informed and made with a sound mind. This is regardless of whether she/he is a Jehovah's Witness. Most of the time, a child would not fulfil this as the child will lack the maturity and capability of forming consent. Hence the courts will have to override the child's desire and order the life-saving blood transfusion to be carried out. However, in the exceptional situation where a child shows sufficient maturity to be able to make an informed decision, the court should not override the child's desire.

<u>*Can consent be genuine and informed?*</u>

First, whether a consent can be genuine and informed must be assessed based on whether the child has made the decision after considering the gravity of the situation. The child must have arrived at an independent, mature judgment that is not heavily influenced by his or her parents' desire. This is a very high threshold to be reached, and most children will lack the necessary maturity level to be able to reach an independent, informed decision regarding a matter of life and death. Hence, in the interest of the child and to ensure that the child continues to live, it is always in the best interest for the court to override the child's apparent wishes and to order the life-saving treatment to be carried out. The actual age of the child does not matter as much as the level of maturity displayed by the child, as different children mature differently; a 14-year-old may be able to show the maturity level of an adult and vice versa.

Exceptions
Second, if the child has shown sufficient maturity and capability to make an informed decision of upholding one's religious belief and refusing to accept a blood transfusion, the court should not order the blood transfusion to be carried out. This is because an invasive surgery such as a blood transfusion should never be carried out against a patient's wishes as this would be intruding on the patient's autonomy to his or her own body and doing so might constitute a crime as the patient would be deliberately harmed in the process against their consent.

This is similar to patients being able to opt out of potentially life-saving operations if they refuse to be treated for various reasons. For example, they might not want to drag out their suffering if they are suffering from a terminal illness, or they do not want to run the risk of the operation failing. It is under the doctors' Hippocratic Oath to act in the patient's best interests, but the patient's consent ultimately still trumps any potential operation that can be done on the patient Hence, a stringent test will have to be carried out to ensure that the child has made an informed and independent decision, and as explained above this will be a very high threshold to establish to prevent abuse.

Hence, it is nearly always the case that the court should order the life-saving blood transfusion to be carried out on the child, subject to the exceptional circumstance where it can be established that the threshold has been established and the child has made an independent and informed decision not to accept the blood transfusion.

Examiner's Comments:

Overall: This response provides a nuanced and analytical approach to the question., The writer also made a very sensible suggestion as to why there might be exceptional circumstances where we might have to accept that the child refuses to receive the blood transfusion. Due to the added level of analysis and nuance, this essay will score well.

Introduction: The introduction directly answers the question and clearly sets out the two main arguments that will be raised in the main body, hence showing the candidate has thought about how to structure his or her essay before writing it out.

Main Body: The two main paragraphs deal with two distinct points that have been elaborated in detail and has shown a very deep level of analysis. Again, this is another example of quality over quantity, even though this response has only raised two main arguments as opposed to the previous response, the level of deeper analysis is preferred over a shallow treatment of many different points.

Conclusion: The conclusion nicely summarises the candidate's argument and reminds the examiner why there might be exceptional circumstances where the court should allow the child to refuse the blood transfusion.

Worse response:

The court should never allow someone to refuse a blood transfusion because a person's life is more important than one's religious beliefs. Therefore, if the blood transfusion was life-saving, the child should not be able to refuse it on the grounds of religion.

Life is sacrosanct and without the right to live, the child would not be able to enjoy other rights, such as right to religious freedom. Hence, in such a scenario where the right to pursue one's religious beliefs directly conflicts with one's right to live, the right to live takes precedence and the child should not be allowed to refuse the blood transfusion.

There is also the issue of the child being too young to be able to decide what religion he or she wishes to adhere to. This risks the child not having a say regarding whether to receive a life-saving treatment. The child may just be repeating what his or her parents have told him or her regarding their religious belief without forming an independent thought as to whether the belief is so important that they should refuse a life-saving treatment.

Even though the parents have parental control over the child, parents do not have absolute control over their children's lives. For example, parents are not allowed to harm their children. Hence, if the parents convinced the child that their religious belief disallows any form of blood transfusion even though it is a life-saving treatment, this is tantamount to harming the child. This puts the child at risk of dying. In the interest of the child's life, the court should override the parents' wishes and allow the hospital to let the child undergo a blood transfusion to save the child's life.

Even though we live in a society that tolerates religious freedom and expression, we should draw a line when doing so results in harm and danger to a child. This is a case where the right to freedom of expression of religion causes an actual risk to a child's life, and hence we cannot tolerate such an expression of religious freedom because the child's life has absolute priority.

Therefore, in conclusion, the court should not allow the child to refuse consent to the blood transfusion and the child's life takes priority over the child's religion.

Examiner's Comments:

Overall: This is a reasonable attempt at tackling the question, and this essay answers the question directly. It comes across as being slightly one-sided at times, and the candidate could have achieved higher marks by addressing the counter-arguments more in order to bolster his or her own argument. The structure is clear enough for the examiner to follow the candidate's argument. Overall, this essay will achieve an above average mark of 4 to 5.

Introduction: The introduction answers the question and hence provides a good starting point. However, the candidate should also have taken this opportunity to set out the main arguments that will be expanded on in the main body so that the examiner knows from the outset what will be the three main points raised by the candidate.

Main Body: The main body sets out three points with some analysis and explanation. As mentioned above, more could be done with regards to raising counter-arguments and addressing them effectively, to not make the essay overly one-sided. Headings could also be used in this case to set out clearly what the three main points are since this has not already been done in the introduction.

Conclusion: The conclusion summarises the candidate's main argument.

EXAMPLE ESSAY 4

Think about the different kinds of contracts that are made in everyday life and explain how they are formed and how they are enforceable.

Better response:

There are different types of contracts made in everyday life. First, there are from simple, bilateral contracts such as a contract between a supplier and a customer. Second, there are complex, multilateral contracts such as a multi-million project involving numerous parties. These contracts are usually formed by parties signing their names on the written contract to indicate their intention to enter into a contract and be bound.

Simple contracts

Simple contracts are made in everyday life and may sometimes not even be blatantly obvious to the parties entering into the contract. For example, when you purchase a laptop and agree to the terms and conditions online, you are effectively entering into a contract with the supplier. By checking the box, you are indicating your agreement to be bound by the terms of the contract. The fault is on the buyer if they fail to check the terms properly before entering into the agreement. However, because of the imbalance of power between the supplier and the regular consumer (the supplier tends to be more sophisticated), the law has stepped in to ensure that consumers are not exploited and there are implied terms to the effect that such terms must not be onerous and unfair to the consumer.

Complex contracts

On the other end of the spectrum, we have complex, multi-lateral contracts involving several parties. Another feature of such contracts is that they tend to provide a benefit and detriment to both parties. This means that one party stands to gain money by providing a service, hence the money gained is the benefit and the effort needed to provide the service is a detriment. However, there are also contracts that are formed by the lack of a written agreement, such as by express oral agreement.

For example, in large commercial transactions, you will usually expect multiple parties to be involved. This could include banks, corporations and institutional investors. Such parties tend to be extremely sophisticated and will ensure that the written contract encompasses all the rights and obligations that are available to each party. Hence, the law will have less leeway to impose implied conditions. An example of an implied condition would be to provide third parties with rights if they have relied on the contract. The sophisticated commercial parties will also ensure that any external communication or documentation will not affect the rights and obligations laid out in the written contract to ensure there is commercial certainty, hence they will tend to include a whole agreement provision.

<u>Oral agreements</u>
Even though written contracts are the most common form of contracts, the law has ensured that express oral agreements will be held to be binding if there is an intention to form a contract. For example, if you agree to purchase something over the phone with a supplier, you are held to have entered into an agreement and if you go back on your word, the supplier has an enforceable contract against you. This is something that is actively excluded by commercial parties as they will almost always insist on a written contract for commercial certainty.

Hence, contracts can be formed either orally or by written agreement, with the latter being the overwhelmingly most common form of contract. Contracts are enforceable as they contain rights and obligations binding on both parties. If one party breaches the obligations of the contract, the other party will have an actionable claim.

Examiner's Comments:

Overall: This is a good attempt at handling this broad question. For such broad questions, it is up to the candidate to demonstrate that they can think of different situations involving a contract. This includes more novel situations such as oral agreements as opposed to the standard written contract. There is also a good attempt at explaining the different elements behind the formation and enforcement of a contract. This essay will achieve a mark of 7 to 8.

Introduction: The introduction clearly sets out the different kinds of contracts that the candidate wishes to elaborate on in the main body and sets out nicely the different elements involved.

Main Body: The three main paragraphs provide three distinct points that have been elaborated to a sufficient standard. The level of analysis is also very good considering that no prior legal knowledge is required.

Conclusion: The conclusion provides a good summary of the different kinds of contracts and how they are formed, and helps the examiner understand what the candidate understands from the question.

Worse response:

I can think of many contracts that I frequently enter into in my everyday life – when I take up a job and have to sign an employment contract, when I enter into a phone contract, and when I have to sign a rental agreement in my university.

For these contracts, they have all been prepared by the other party. I did not get much of a say regarding their terms and conditions. There are usually very lengthy clauses, but from my experience so far the main clauses usually include things such as price (e.g. wage, price of the phone or amount of rent payable), duration (e.g. length of employment, length of phone contract and length of rental agreement) and certain provisions detailing the rights and obligations of both parties. I would say that these contracts are formed as soon as I sign the contract and hand it back to the other party, as signing a contract indicates my consent to be bound by the contract.

On the other hand, I think such contracts are enforceable whenever one party commits a mistake that is prohibited by the contract. For example, I have heard of people who get fired from their jobs because they have done something prohibited by their employment contract, such as not turning up on time or not wearing the correct attire. Similarly, we might lose our rental deposit if we breach our rental agreement, such as damaging the room or not adhering to the house rules. Hence, we must be careful in reading the terms of the contract to ensure we do not breach it as we might become liable under the contract.

These contracts can be useful as they usually provide a benefit, for example by signing an employment contract I get to receive a wage in return for working for the employer. As for a phone contract, they usually allow me to purchase a phone at a cheaper price in return for being bound under the same telecommunication company for a period. As for a rental agreement, they allow us to be able to live in a place during university and have access to certain amenities in return for paying rent.

Overall, contracts in everyday life usually provide a benefit if you adhere to the conditions. They can be used for several purposes, such as the three examples I have mentioned.

Examiner's Comments:

Overall: This is a distinctly different style of writing from the previous response. Whilst not wrong, it comes across as being less academic-like than the previous response. This style is not fatal to the marks the essay will receive if it answers the question, which this response does. What is lacking is a deeper level of analysis of the different kinds of contracts that might be available and the elements behind the formation and enforcement of a contract, as this response provides a rather superficial and simplistic level of thought. Overall, this essay will likely score a mark of 4 or 5.

Introduction: The sets out the different kinds of contracts the candidate wishes to elaborate out, which is satisfactory. However, the candidate could have also mentioned the different elements involved in the formation and enforcement of a contract.

Main Body: The three main paragraphs all elaborate on a different example that the candidate raised, so the structure is fine and works well. However, as mentioned, the level of analysis is insufficient. The candidate would have done better by showing a deeper level of thought and included more novel forms of contracts that may be created differently.

Conclusion: The conclusion is satisfactory and provides an acceptable summary of the candidate's arguments.

EXAMPLE ESSAY 5

In what situations should we prevent a contract from being unenforceable, and in what situations should judges have more power in making a contract enforceable?

Better response:

Contracts should be unenforceable if they lack the formalities required to constitute a contract: if there is a lack of intention to create a contractual relationship, if there is a lack of consideration, or if it goes against public policy such as being unfair to a weaker party or being illegal. On the other hand, courts have the powers to enforce an otherwise unenforceable contract if there is a defect in formalities, for example if the wording is unclear, and the courts will have to adhere to the tests of business necessity and efficiency.

Contracts demand formalities because this provides commercial certainty and ensures that there is a clear display of intention to enter a formal contractual relationship. Hence, for example, a contract needs to be signed by both parties to signify their intention to enter into an agreement. If there is a clear lack of formality, for example one party did not sign the agreement, we cannot enforce this contract as it will show a lack of intention from one party to enter into a contract, as a contract requires the consent of both parties.

A lack of consideration is also fatal to the existence of a contract under English law. For example, a gratuitous contract stating that one party will give another party a certain sum of money in exchange of nothing will not be enforceable and will be constituted as a gift. This is because a party cannot be obliged to hand over a gift if he does not incur any benefit from the transaction. This is due to public policy reasons in order to prevent individuals from being forced to carry out the gifts that they may have promised to do so.

Unfair contracts should also be unenforceable if they are made against a weaker party. For example, an employee in an employer-employee relationship and a consumer in a supplier-consumer relationship. This is because the weaker party often do not get to dictate any of the terms of the contract. The law should protect the weaker party by preventing the stronger party from imposing unfair conditions. For example, a condition that prevents a consumer from being able to bring a complaint if the good is below a reasonable standard will not be enforceable.

Illegal contracts are also unenforceable due to public policy reasons. For example, a contract that purports to flout an environmental law will not be enforceable. Parties cannot enter obligations that will cause them to commit an offence.

Judges have the power to enforce certain contracts that might be deemed unenforceable. For example, a badly drafted contract might result in the obligations of the parties being unclear. However, in the interest of commercial certainty and to ensure that the parties' wishes are not frustrated due to an unclear wording, the judges have the power to imply terms into the contract that will make it workable. For example, the judges can look at the whole contract and imply a term out of business necessity. Similarly, if both parties have indicated at the outset that they agree that the contracts contain a certain obligation, but they forgot to include this condition, the judges can imply such an obligation. Hence, this will ensure that contracts do not become enforceable due to a drafting error or mistake and this will preserve commercial certainty.

In conclusion, contracts should not be enforceable if they lack the elements needed to form a contract. These include the relevant formalities, consideration and intent to create legal relations. On the other hand, certain formality defects can be forgiven if the judge is able to imply terms to the effect of preserving the parties' intentions.

Examiner's Comments:

Overall: This is a good response. The candidate not only talks about the elements behind the creation of a contract and why a lack of any element might make a contract enforceable, the candidate has also provided a decent analysis of how judges might go about making a contract enforceable and the reason behind them doing so. This would achieve an 8.

Introduction: The introduction is good and sets out the main arguments the candidate will elaborate on, providing a good roadmap for the examiner to follow.

Main Body: The separate paragraphs all raise a distinct point and there is a good level of analysis for most of the points mentioned. The candidate does raise many different points but the candidate has shown that he or she is able to talk in more detail for the harder issues raised. For example, the judge's ability to imply terms into the contract, hence the candidate has shown that he or she is able to understand the question to a good extent and to elaborate accordingly using relevant examples.

Conclusion: The conclusion is good and sums up the candidate's arguments in a clear and coherent manner.

Worse response:

We should not enforce contracts if they are unfair or if they are illegal. On the contrary, judges should enforce contracts that are genuinely entered into as it will be unfair on the party who has relied on the contract if it becomes unenforceable.

Contracts are unfair if they purport to impose onerous obligations on either party. For example, if an employer forces an employee to work long hours and provides insufficient benefits, such as not providing paid sick leave or not providing adequate salary, such a contract should be unenforceable. Unfair contracts that prevent consumers from enforcing their rights should also be unenforceable, such as contracts not allowing consumers to exchange or refund defective products. Rental contracts that demand an exorbitant deposit or overly restrict a tenant's ability to live in the apartment should also be unenforceable.

Illegal contracts should also be rendered unenforceable as they go against the rule of law and such contracts should not be entered into in the first place. For example, contracts of prostitution should not be enforceable, unless prostitution is legal in a particular jurisdiction. Similarly, contracts to supply drugs should not be enforceable. Finally, contracts to assassinate someone or to harm someone will never be enforceable. Hence, these are all examples of illegal contracts that should not be enforceable.

The courts should have greater powers to enforce contracts that have been entered into the parties. For example, if an employer agrees to pay an employee a certain wage in return for providing labour, the courts should exercise their powers in enforcing the contract. Even if there is a lack of a formal written contract, if the employee has relied on the employer's promise and provided a benefit to the employer in terms of providing labour. Similarly, if a written contract is badly drafted, the courts should exercise its powers to enforce the contract if both parties were clear from the outset what the obligations of the contract were.

In summary, unfair and illegal contracts should not be enforceable as they will produce injustice and go against the rule of law. On the flip side, contracts that are made with lack of formalities should be enforceable by the courts provided both parties had a clear intent of entering into a contract.

Examiner's Comments:

Overall: This is a decent attempt at the question – it answers the question well and provides relevant examples and elaboration to support its argument. The analysis is sufficient but in order to achieve high marks a deeper analysis would be preferred. The structure is clear and easy to follow. This would achieve a 6 or 7.

Introduction: The introduction is very clear and sets out the main examples and arguments that will be put forward in the main body.

Main Body: The examples given and elaborated on are valid and there are no major errors in the candidate's analysis. If the candidate went on further to analyse why certain types of contracts might be unenforceable, and the more nuanced examples of why the courts might have to step in to make a contract enforceable due to the lack of formalities, the candidate would have achieved an even stronger mark.

Conclusion: The conclusion is good and provides an adequate summary of the candidate's arguments and wraps up the essay nicely.

EXAMPLE ESSAY 6

To what extent should we protect someone's right to live at a particular place?

Better response:

A person's right to live at a particular place should be protected to the extent that the person has a legal right to the property, failing which we should look at whether the person has acquired any equitable proprietary right in the property that is not defeated by a strong legal right of another person. If the person has a family life in the property, this would also be a factor that weighs in favour of the person's right to live in the property being protected as a person's family life should not be disrupted unless there is a good public policy reason to do so.

A person has a legal right to the property if they have purchased the property and are registered as the legal owners of the property. Such individuals have the strongest right available and can defeat any other claims to the property. Hence, the legal owners have the security of legal title and their rights to live at the property will be protected to the fullest extent, save for the extraordinary scenario where the government needs to acquire the land for development purposes, which in that case the legal owners need to be adequately compensated to ensure that they are given a suitable alternative property of equal or higher value.

If a person does not enjoy legal right to the property, their rights should only be protected to the extent they have an equitable proprietary right to the property. For example, the person's name was never registered under the legal title or the person is only living in the property as a tenant. A tenant's rights are determined by the terms of the leasehold agreement, which will clearly state the length of their occupancy and the facilities available to them.

However, beyond the leasehold agreement, such tenants have an expectation that their right to live in the property is protected adequately even though they are not legal owners. For example, they cannot just be evicted at will by the landlord if the landlord wants to acquire the property back even though the landlord is the legal owner. The law will ensure that adequate notice must be served with a valid reason as to why the landlord wishes to acquire the property back.

Other equitable proprietary rights include squatters that have lived in a property for a sufficiently long period of time – however they face a high threshold as they have to ensure that the owner has not opposed the squatter living in the property throughout the period and the period is made sufficiently long to ensure that the owners are given an opportunity to reject the squatters.

Lastly, family life is a fundamental human right and if someone enjoys a family life in a particular property, the law should ensure that such a right is protected and not disrupted unless there are exceptional circumstances. For example, following a divorce, the wife and her kids may continue living in a property. Even though the husband may be the legal owner of the property, his ability to sell the property will be restricted by the courts if the wife and children enjoy a family life in the property. This is a situation where a legal owner's rights may be curtailed because another individual may enjoy a right to family life that will only be disrupted in exceptional circumstances.

In conclusion, the right to live in a particular property ranges from the strongest legal right to equitable rights. Equitable rights might be defeasible by stronger rights, and subject to human rights such as right to family life that creates an exception to stronger rights.

Examiner's Comments:

Overall: This is a strong attempt at handling the seemingly broad question – the analysis of the relevant law involved and the different classes of rights and exceptions that might apply is excellent and the examples given are very relevant and illustrate a good understanding of the question raised. This would score an 8 or 9.

Introduction: The introduction is effectively written and sets out clearly the points that will be raised subsequently and the different levels of rights and exceptions involved.

Main Body: The structure is good and the candidate has separated out the different classes of rights nicely and has explained sufficiently what each of them might entail. The candidate has provided a good level of analysis of the different forms of rights behind living in a property and in what situations exceptions might apply.

Conclusion: The conclusion is well-written and provides a good summary of the arguments raised by the candidate and reminds the examiner of the main issues raised by the question.

Worse response:

We should firstly protect someone's right to live at a place if they have paid their rent and have been good at observing the rules of their accommodation. If a student has paid their rent, they expect to be able to live in the accommodation throughout their academic year and should not be kicked out as this would cause a lot of problems and be disruptive towards the student's education. The only reason why a student should be kicked out is if the student has flagrantly breached the agreement by damaging the property or illegally subletting the room, otherwise the student's right to live in the accommodation should be protected once rent has been paid.

A family living in a flat should also be protected, and the law should offer some help in the family runs into problems paying rent. For example, a low-income family may experience difficulties keeping up with rent payment, and an unscrupulous landlord may threaten to evict them and pressurise them to pay rent.

However, if the family has children to support, they will be rendered homeless if the landlord can easily evict them due to failure to pay rent. The law should step in and ensure that the right of the family to live in the property is protected as much as possible and they are given an opportunity to maybe defer rent payment and as a last resort, be offered alternative housing at a cheaper price so their family life is protected.

The right to live in a particular property should also be protected if there is some sentimental value attached to the property. The government cannot just acquire a plot of land and uproot someone's right to live somewhere if that person has sentimental value attached to the land, for example the land might have been inherited for generations, or it is in a particular neighbourhood that the person has formed close community ties with. This should be left undisturbed as much as possible, and the government should only be able to acquire the land in very exceptional scenarios, such as if that land is crucial for public safety.

Examiner's Comments:

Overall: This is a weaker attempt than the first response, as the issues raised are largely rather superficial and there is insufficient in depth analysis of the different levels of rights that might be attached to a property, as well as the exceptions that might apply. The structure also suffers from a lack of a proper introduction and conclusion. This essay does answer the question to a certain extent; hence it will be a weak passing mark of 5.

Introduction: There is a lack of introduction and the candidate jumps straight into elaborating on the main body. While the essay is still relatively easy to follow, the lack of a good introduction causes some marks to be lost due to the lack of a good structure.

Main Body: The main body is acceptable as the points are separately paragraphed and relevant examples are given. A stronger analysis would have scored higher marks as it would have shown that the candidate has given greater thought to the question and think about how rights to a property may be more nuanced and layered.

Conclusion: There is a lack of a proper conclusion, again affecting the structure and clarity of the essay and hence the marks will suffer because of the bad structure.

EXAMPLE ESSAY 7

EU law contains two fundamental economic principles – freedom of movement of goods and freedom of movement of people. Discuss how might laws be put in place to achieve these two freedoms.

Better response:

The freedom of movement of persons and goods are both fundamental economic principles behind EU law. They ensure deeper integration between the EU member states by increasing their economic interdependence. Hence, the law ensures that these principles are promoted by removing artificial barriers to trade such as tariffs and custom duties for goods, as well as allowing workers to work freely in the member states and have a right to live and work in a member state and enjoy the social welfare benefits given to workers.

Free movement of goods

The free movement of goods necessitates that a domestic supplier is not given an advantage over a supplier from a different member state because of the different in tariffs and custom duties imposed. For example, if the domestic supplier and the foreign supplier are both supplying the exact same good, the domestic supplier will have an unfair advantage if a hefty tariff and custom duty is imposed on the imported good. In order to promote free movement of goods, the law ensures that such tariffs and custom duties are removed, except for certain protected goods such as defence equipment and goods affecting public health policy such as alcohol. In addition, quotas will also be disallowed as this creates an artificial barrier to entry by preventing foreign suppliers from exporting goods into the member state beyond a certain level.

Free movement of persons

In terms of free movement of persons, the law must ensure that EU citizens are able to freely work in any member state without artificial restrictions. Hence, they can move to another member state and find a job there without facing additional bureaucracy such as applying for a visa or being restricted in living in another member state to seek a job.

They should be entitled to the same benefits that a citizen of the member state enjoys, such as jobseeker's allowance and being allowed access to job-seeking services.

This is subject to exceptions, such as certain standards being put in place to ensure that the EU citizens do not exploit the welfare system of a member state, and they have shown a genuine willingness and effort to look for a job.

Hence, in conclusion, EU law primarily ensures that the two fundamental economic principles of free movement of persons and goods are upheld by removing artificial barriers to entry. For example, removing import tariffs, quotas and custom duties. These fundamental principles also promote the right to live and work in any member state by removing the need for visas, allowing access to jobseeker benefits and enjoying the right to live subject to a test of a genuine willingness to look for a job to prevent an abuse of the member state's welfare system.

Examiner's Comments:

Overall: This is a decent attempt as the candidate has shown a decent understanding of the free movement of persons and goods and how EU law works in general. The essay has room for improvement in terms of providing a more detailed analysis of the different legal tools involved in upholding the free movement of goods and person, but this is a solid attempt and would score a 7.

Introduction: The introduction is effective and setting out two main arguments that will be raised by the candidate and provides a clear structure going forward, showing an attempt in planning.

Main Body: The two paragraphs provide an adequate explanation and analysis of the two freedom of movements mentioned in the question. Perhaps a stronger analysis and evaluation of the different legal tools that can be involved, such as the notion of the EU courts evaluating national laws based on proportionality, will have helped the essay achieve even better marks.

Conclusion: The conclusion is good and provides a good summary of the candidate's analysis of the question.

Worse response:

The laws can ensure free movement of goods and people by ensuring that there are no restrictions in place for selling goods and for travelling, hence someone should be free to buy and sell goods as well as move around without facing any restriction.

Free movement of goods can be encouraged by ensuring that someone is able to buy and sell goods without facing legal restrictions such as additional bureaucracy or high taxes. If someone had to fill in a lot of paperwork or had to pay a hefty tax before buying or selling a good, they will be hindered from doing so and this will reduce the freedom of movement of goods.

Another way free movement of goods can be encouraged is to promote the free sale of goods. Hence, the laws should encourage goods to be sold easily on the market and should protect the rights of sellers. Sellers should be able to freely sell their goods at any location without being hindered by regulations or specific requirement. For example, laws that restrict certain goods from being sold in a specific market should be relaxed to promote free movement of goods.

As for the free movement of persons, such movement can be encouraged by the laws making it easier and cheaper for people to move around. For example, visa-free travel will encourage people to move around with less restrictions. There should also be less regulations in working in different markets as this will allow people to move around more freely. There should also be laws allowing someone to bring over their family to a new location so that there are lesser obstacles in preventing a person from moving around freely.

The above points are the ways in which the law can promote freedom of movement of goods and persons.

Examiner's Comments:

Overall: This is a weak attempt as it shows that candidate has not truly understood the question. The points made miss the mark in terms of what the issues raised by the question. For a niche topic like this, candidates should only attempt such a question if they have read up about the topic and have an idea about the issues that are potentially raised in this question. Since the question has not been answered according to what is being asked, this will achieve a failing mark of 4.

Introduction: The introduction is simple but does not add much. It does not provide clarity in structure and does not set out the key arguments that will be raised by the candidate. Hence, it does not add more marks to the essay in terms of showing a clear structure and adequate planning.

Main Body: The candidate fails to truly grapple with the question asked and has not shown a good level of analysis in terms of the principle behind free movement of goods and persons under EU law. The suggestions given are rather superficial, such as focusing on tourism under free movement of persons when more emphasis should have been given on the freedom of EU citizens to work in any EU member state.

Conclusion: The conclusion is inadequate as it simply states that the points have been made in the main body. It does not add any value to the essay. Candidates should make use of the conclusion to remind the examiner of the arguments that have been raised and to wrap up the essay nicely so that the examiner can fully understand the points raised by the candidate.

EXAMPLE ESSAY 8

Should there be greater legal restrictions in companies making use of offshore tax structures?

Better response:

This essay will argue that making use of offshore tax structures should be restricted to the extent that companies are evading tax instead of structuring their businesses efficiently in order to minimise tax liability. This is a fine line and arguably the level of legal restrictions currently put in place do not go far enough in reducing the risk of companies abusing offshore tax structures.

If a company principally benefits from doing business in the UK, they should be subject to corporation tax as any other business would be. They cannot simply evade taxes by channelling their profits away towards an offshore jurisdiction with low tax liability. This would not be problematic if the company a multinational and has businesses split between different regions, including regions with lower tax liability. However, the law needs to be stricter in ensuring that companies are more transparent regarding their business operations and how much profit is made in each jurisdiction. This way, companies will be less likely to abuse offshore jurisdictions in reducing their tax liability and give them an unfair advantage over other companies that pay corporation tax in the UK.

There is a fine line between tax evasion and tax avoidance. The law needs to be clearer regarding when the line is breached. There are accounting rules and disclosure requirements put in place for companies to ensure that they financial statements and accounts are subject to scrutiny and audit to ensure that they are not engaged in any illegal tax avoidance schemes. Instances where the law should regard a scheme is legal include situations where a company is diversifying its operations overseas and has a genuine commercial reason for having a presence in an overseas jurisdiction. On the flip side of the coin, instances where such a scheme should be illegal is when a company creates a shell company in an offshore jurisdiction just to take advantage of the lower taxes, without having any business activity in the offshore jurisdiction.

The law does not go far enough to regulate the usage of offshore tax structures because it has been shown from time and time again through the Panama Papers and Paradise Papers that large companies are able to reduce their tax liability by a very substantial amount without falling under the scrutiny of the tax authorities and without getting into any trouble. This shows an unsatisfactory loophole in the taxation laws, and the law arguably needs to make it harder for companies to artificially depress their tax liability to a point where it is not proportionate to the benefits they receive from having a presence and doing business in a particular jurisdiction.

In conclusion, the law needs to close the loopholes currently present in our taxation laws so as to make it harder for large companies to artificially lower their tax liability, as well as make it clearer what falls under tax avoidance and what falls under tax evasion.

Examiner's Comments:

Overall: This is a decent attempt at a difficult and technical question, and what makes the essay stand out is the usage of relevant examples (the Paradise Papers and the Panama Papers), as well as a good level of understanding of why companies might make use of offshore tax structures and how the law goes about regulating such usage. A good distinction has also been drawn between tax evasion and tax avoidance. Overall, this would score a 7 to 8.

Introduction: The introduction is good and draws the line between tax avoidance and evasion right from the start. It could have perhaps set out more clearly what are the different arguments that will be elaborated on in the main body.

Main Body: The level of understanding and analysis shown regarding the usage of offshore tax structures is good, perhaps not perfect but this is a more than acceptable level of analysis that will be expected since no prior legal knowledge is needed. If the candidate shows he or she has attempted to analyse the question asked and has shown a good level of further reading and understanding, a good mark will be achieved for a difficult and technical question such as this.

Conclusion: The conclusion is good and neatly summarises the main arguments that have been put forward and answers the question again directly.

Worse response:

I feel that it is unfair that big companies get to avoid paying taxes just because they are larger and more experienced and hence can come up with complex schemes. This results in an unfair advantage against small companies, who do not have the capabilities or resources to invest in complex schemes. Hence, the law needs to clamp down on big companies making use of offshore structures to reduce their tax liability.

Big companies have the resources to pay for tax lawyers to come up with sophisticated, elaborate schemes in order to reduce their tax liability. For example, they set up branches in offshore tax havens and channelling their profits to such jurisdictions in order to reduce their tax liability. Furthermore, since big companies that to have many international offices and have a more diversified portfolio, they can cover up their actions more and treat it as a business diversification exercise rather than a tax evasion exercise.

Small companies are disadvantaged because they do not have the capabilities to hire tax lawyers to arrange their finances accordingly to reduce their tax liability. Furthermore, they tend to be more domestic in nature and will not be able to take advantage of having an international network in covering up any potential tax evasion measures as being a lawful business diversification measure.

The law gives too much advantage to big companies when they already have the upper hand as compared to small companies in terms of presence and financial resources. Hence, the law needs to place more onerous measures on big companies such as restricting their ability to channel profits to offshore structures so that these big companies will pay their tax accordingly if small companies must pay such taxes as well.

Examiner's Comments:

Overall: This is also a sensible attempt at tackling a difficult technical question, albeit this response does not show the same level of understanding and analysis as the first response. This response comes across as more simplistic in general, drawing a dividing line between big and small companies and their different in financial power, as opposed to the first response which drew a more nuanced and crucial line between tax evasion and tax avoidance measures. This response will score a 4 to 5.

Introduction: The introduction is acceptable and does set out the main argument the candidate will make. Whilst first person is acceptable, it is not generally that appropriate for academic piece of writing.

Main Body: As explained above, whilst it is good that the candidate has come up with a valid point about the difference in financial power between big and small companies and hence their ability to structure their tax liability accordingly, this analysis is perhaps not exactly what the question was ultimately looking for. The first response comes closer to showing a better understanding by trying to pick apart why tax evasion and tax avoidance may be different and how might the usage of an offshore tax structure fall into either side of the line.

Conclusion: There is a lack of a proper conclusion in this response. This is not fatal as it ultimately does not hinder the examiner's understanding of the essay since the structure has been consistent and clear throughout, but perhaps show a lack of time management and a conclusion might have boosted the essay's marks slightly.

EXAMPLE ESSAY 9

Should historic sexual abuse cases that have happened several decades ago still be enforceable by the prosecution? Discuss.

Better response:

This essay will argue that historic sexual abuse cases should be enforceable only if three conditions are fulfilled. First, the prosecution is confident that the evidence available has not been rendered unreliable due to a lapse of time. Second, the usual standards of 'sufficient evidence to prosecute'. Third, proving a defendant's guilt 'beyond reasonable doubt' should still apply to maintain the integrity of the criminal justice system.

One problem with prosecuting historic sexual abuse cases is that due to a lapse of several decades, witnesses or circumstantial evidence become less reliable. There is a danger of convicting someone with insufficient evidence. This goes against the fundamental tenet of our criminal justice system: a defendant is deemed innocent until proven guilty under the adversarial system. After several decades, any potential witnesses will probably be a lot less like to be available for trial. The possibility of obtaining any DNA evidence or fingerprint evidence would also be negligible. Hence, these cases usually heavily rely on the victim's account of the crime, but without any supporting evidence it provides a very dangerous potential false conviction if the prosecution pursues the case.

We should nevertheless not ignore the fact that victims might often have a good reason for not reporting a crime immediately. Many victims will be under personal distress and immense emotional and physical trauma. Therefore, they might not be in the right state of mind to bring a claim immediately and be subject to a long, arduous trial.

Furthermore, several victims are under an imbalance of power and might not want to harm their career prospects if the perpetrator happens to be their employer or be someone in a position of authority who is influential. These are factors that should be taken into account in deciding whether to pursue a case that has happened decades ago, but this is still subject to the important rule that there must be sufficient evidence to bring a prosecution and the victim's words alone without any supporting evidence from the victim will often be insufficient.

Limitation periods are imposed in law for both civil and criminal claims in order to ensure that the case does not become stale. This ensures evidence does not become unreliable due to the influx of time. Hence, there is a valid reason why sexual abuse cases which have happened decades ago might not always be the most appropriate cases to prosecute. Whilst we should be sympathetic to the victims and not apply limitation rules harshly. They may have very good reasons for not bringing a claim earlier, we should bear the importance of limitation periods in mind and balance the potential injustice done to the victim versus the potential injustice that may be done to an alleged offender if the offender is wrongly accused of a crime that has happened several decades ago.

In conclusion, we should always demand for sufficient evidence to bring a prosecution for a crime that has happened decades ago, and this will unfortunately be difficult for certain cases where the evidence has become unreliable and there is no supporting evidence beyond the victim's testimony.

Examiner's Comments:

Overall: This is a good response and the candidate has shown a deeper level of analysis regarding the purpose of limitation periods. It also talks about the important principles behind the criminal justice system and has balanced these matters in a mature and measured manner. The candidate has also shown a good level of understanding behind evidential matters and has given good relevant examples when appropriate. This would score a 7 or 8.

Introduction: The introduction is good and sets out very in a structured way the key principles of the criminal justice system that permeates the analysis behind the essay. It also sets out the main argument the candidate wishes to make in order to answer the question.

Main Body: The main arguments put forward are all very well thought out, nuanced and sensitive to the topic raised. The candidate has avoided the trap of producing an overly personal, non-academic essay that many candidates may be tempted to produce due to the sensational topic raised by the question. Such a question tends to be very popular but it also where many students will tend to write an essay that is not legalistic and does not show enough analysis to achieve high marks for a CLT essay.

This essay has shown how one can approach a sensitive and sensational issue in a measured and legalistic manner.

Conclusion: The conclusion is good and neatly summarises why the candidate feels we should not readily prosecute historic sexual abuse cases and gives the examiner a good idea of the main reasons behind put forward by the candidate.

Worse response:

Sexual abuse should never be tolerated and someone who has committed a sexual offence should not be let off the hook simply because his offence was not reported for a long time. If there is sufficient evidence to indicate the offence has been committed, such an offence should still be enforceable despite the time lapse.

The problem with reporting sexual offenders is that there are many victims who may be embarrassed or traumatised about the situation. They rather keep the incident under wraps and not report the offence to the authorities. This causes many sexual offenders to be let off the hook. Hence, the law should make it such that these offenders can be held guilty even if an offence is reported many years later, taking into account the fact that sometimes victims might need some time to get over the traumatic incident in order to have the courage to speak up about the abuse.

Another problem is that sexual abuse often occurs when there is an imbalance in power between the offender and the victim. For example, the offender may be an employer of the victim. The offender may also be in a position of authority, such as a teacher or an instructor. In these situations, victims are often afraid of reporting the abuse as they may be afraid of affecting their career or receiving stigma from society. Therefore, many cases only come to light several years after they occur, and it is in the interest of justice that such cases should remain enforceable even if they are only reported several years after the incident has occurred.

The issue of false reports should not be understated. The confidence in the criminal justice system should still be upheld by ensuring that such alleged incidents should only be actively prosecuted if there is enough compelling evidence. This is to tackle the problem of alleged male offenders being wrongly accused, only to be acquitted following many years of trial. This not only damages one's reputation and career but is also potentially emotionally distressing and adequate safeguards should be put in place to ensure that there is confidence in the system.

Examiner's Comments:

Overall: This is a decent response to a question that has received a lot of press attention lately. It is likely to be a popular question since many candidates would have read up about it. This essay comes across as slightly one-sided initially with not enough legal analysis of the reason why cases that have occurred several decades ago may not be suitable for prosecution, but the final paragraph sort of address the counter-argument behind prosecuting such alleged offences too readily and balances out the essay. More legal analysis regarding the limitation periods of crimes would have helped this essay score a higher mark. This would score a 5 to 6.

Introduction: The introduction is acceptable and sets out the candidate's main argument, but it should have set out the key points the candidate was going to elaborate in the main body to provide the examiner with a clear road map to understand the essay.

Main Body: The analysis in the first two paragraphs is valid but as mentioned above, they come across as being overly one-sided. The candidate should have addressed the counter-argument of not readily allowing historic sexual abuse cases to be prosecuted because the lapse of time might have rendered the evidence less reliable. The last paragraph is good and shows that the candidate has thought about addressing the counter-arguments and the candidate has made a sensible suggestion to balance out an otherwise heavily one-sided essay.

Conclusion: There is no proper conclusion in this case, hence once again the candidate should have summed up his or her argument concisely in order to potentially score extra points for clarity and structure.

EXAMPLE ESSAY 10

Do you think a child can have more than two parents? Discuss.

Better response:

This essay will argue that a child can have more than two parents. A child can only ever have two genetic parents (with the rare exception of the DNA of three parents being mixed to produce a child, but that is very new technology). However, allowing a child to have more than two parents may more accurately reflect the reality of family life. We have moved on from a society which focus on having two opposite-sex parents and we have increasingly recognised the fact that there are many alternative family units, such as single-parent families, and there is no compelling reason why we should not recognise family units with more than two parents.

<u>Two parents</u>
We cannot change the fact that most of the time, a child will have the genes of two opposite-sex parents. These parents will obviously be the genetic parents of the child. Currently however, sometimes a genetic parent will not be a legal parent, with mechanisms such as sperm donation, surrogacy and adoption.

<u>Sperm donor</u>
A sperm donor fundamentally has no legal claim to be a parent of the child at all, as it is standard protocol. In line with legal regulations that the sperm donor will waive all rights to the child and agree not to have any contact with the legal parents or child after donating his sperm. Hence, even though technically the sperm donor is a 'third parent' as he is a genetic father, the legal parents will still be the mother who gave birth to the child and the father who is married to the mother.

Surrogate

This matter is complicated with surrogacy agreements. While the genetic parents may be the same people as the legal parents, a surrogate mother was used to carry the child through pregnancy. The surrogate mother is a gestational mother of the child as she gives birth to the child. However, the child will not have the genetic material of the surrogate mother. In jurisdictions that recognise surrogacy agreements, such a mother may have also waived all her rights similarly to a sperm donor, but in countries with tighter regulations behind surrogacy agreements it may be illegal to waive a surrogate mother's rights to the child without her informed consent even after the child is born.

This is hence another situation where the surrogate mother may be a 'third parent' in the sense of being a gestational mother, but also potentially a legal parent in certain jurisdictions.

Adoption

Lastly, adoption effectively transfers legal parenthood from the original legal and genetic parents to the foster parents who become the new legal parents of the child. This creates a situation where a child seemingly has two sets of parents. Even though the original parents will waive their rights to the child under an adoption agreement, there are several situations where the child will re-establish communication with their original parents upon adulthood. Hence, despite the child only having one set of parents in legal terms, the reality shows that the child is more akin to having two set of parents.

In conclusion, the idea of a family unit is constantly changing, and the law adapts in reaction to the different ideas of what constitutes a family and whom can be considered a 'parent' of the child. There are different forms of parents, and hence it is not necessarily always the case that a child can only have two parents.

Examiner's Comments:

Overall: This is a very good response and the candidate has shown a high level of analysis in terms of explaining the nuances behind different forms of parenthood and how legal parenthood may differ from genetic parenthood for example. The candidate has also provided many good relevant examples and elaborated on them in detail. They can show that there are many exceptions to the default rule that a child has two parents. Overall, this is a very good attempt and this essay would score an 8 or 9.

Introduction: The introduction is good and provides a good starting point for the candidate to elaborate in more detail why there are many exceptions to the default rule. A slight improvement can be made to the introduction by setting out the main arguments that are going to be made in the main body in order to provide a clearer structure.

Main Body: The examples given and the accompanying explanation and analysis are very precise and shows a high level of understanding regarding the notion of parenthood and the different forms of family units that might be available. This is a question that is easy for candidates to trip up if they muddle the issue of parenthood and fail to provide a good analysis of the different forms of family units. Hence, this candidate has stood out by being clear, precise and coherent in his or her analysis.

Conclusion: Good punchy conclusion that provides a nice closure to the arguments and examples that have been raised so far.

Worse response:

I think all children should have two parents as studies have shown that a stable family unit is highly beneficial for a child's development and progress. This is something that might be beyond one's control, for example a spouse may have died or a divorce inevitably happens, but a child should ideally have two parents to provide him or her with a good foundation.

Studies have shown children in single-parent families often face a greater risk of truancy, lower grades and a higher risk of developing bad habits later in life. There is a direct correlation between a stable family unit and a child's potential achievement later in life. Hence, as much as possible, a child should have two parents to provide support.

Maybe in some cases a child can have more than two 'parents', for example not everyone will be born in a stable family unit with two loving parents, hence in many cases the people providing support for a child may be the grandparents, or uncles and aunts who might be taking care of the child. Such individuals may assume the role of a 'parent' or takeover the parents' duties if they are not up to it, and these children have an equal chance of having a stable environment to learn and develop and grow up to be successful.

Ultimately, there is a special bond between the child and his two parents in terms of their familial ties and this should not be taken lightly. There is a special symbolic nature behind a child and a parent's genetic lineage, hence even if we might accept the fact that sometimes the de facto parents of a child are different from the actual parents, and may involve more than two people, the two actual parents of a child will still hold a special place.

Hence, it is submitted that we can recognise situations of more than two de facto parents, but the real parents of a child will always be the two genetic parents.

Examiner's Comments:

Overall: This essay misses the point of the question and does not provide a sufficient legalistic analysis of the question asked and does not go far enough in dissecting the different concepts of parenthood. The sentences are also too long and convoluted. It is uncontroversial that there are almost always two genetic parents, what the examiner would like to see for such a question is for a candidate to provide a deeper analysis of how might the law consider a child to have more than two parents beyond a superficial description of the genetic ties. This would be a failing mark of 3.

Introduction: The introduction is acceptable ignoring the fact that the content of the essay misses the mark. There is a direct answering of the question, but perhaps briefly outlining the main arguments that will be made would have helped in terms of structure and clarity.

Main Body: The main points raised are rather superficial and are not up to the level of legal exposition that is expected for a CLT essay. Even though no prior legal knowledge is expected, the examiner would like to see a decent attempt at thinking about what the question is truly asking and why might the law want to recognise more than two parents. There is no mention in this essay about alternative family units beyond generic observations about grandparents and relatives taking care of a child, and how the idea of a family unit has shifted over time with different procreation methods.

Conclusion: The conclusion is acceptable but ignores the fact that the content could be improved on to score a better mark.

EXAMPLE ESSAY 11

To what extent do you think international law shapes English law?

Better response:

This essay will argue that international law shapes English law to the extent that Parliament enacts statutes in accordance with the international law obligations that they adhere to. This includes fundamental international law obligations such as observing conventions against torture and child trafficking. I will also argue that international law shapes English law to the extent that judges are able to refer to the UK's international law obligations in deciding certain constitutional cases, such as deciding whether certain human rights are given adequate protection when assessing the level of protection recommended by international law conventions.

The UK regularly enters into international law obligations that are binding. For example, being a signatory to conventions related to genocide, greenhouse gas emissions and human trafficking. These conventions are usually entered into by many different sovereign states. There is an expectation that the countries adhere to the international law standards and amend their laws accordingly to enforce such standards. Hence, Parliament has the prerogative to amend or enact new statutes accordingly in order to give effect to such international law obligations. However, English law and international law belong on separate plane., Hence, international law will only ever become part of English law when Parliament enacts it as statute. This means that judges will not be able to enforce an international law obligation if it is not part of a statute.

There are arguments to the effect that there are certain international law obligations that are so fundamental that they automatically form part of English law and hence are directly enforceable. For example, conventions pertaining to the prohibition against torture and slavery can be regarded as fundamental human rights that should automatically be respected and no derogation should be permitted whatsoever.

However, international law is a different form of law as there is no central legislative authority under international law that oversees making laws and hence there is no concept of parliamentary sovereignty under international law. Hence, under English law, parliamentary sovereignty remains with the English Parliament and such international law obligations will only become part of English law upon being incorporated under statute.

There are certain constitutional cases where judges may refer to international law obligations, such as the obligation to prevent discrimination. However, judges are ultimately still bound by statute and have no legislative ability beyond the limited powers conferred on them in terms of handing down binding decisions in the common law system. Hence, it is still the case that international law obligations may influence judiciary decisions and sway their opinion accordingly. However, they are ultimately still bound by statutory provisions and a change in law to keep it in line with international law obligations can only be done by Parliament.

In conclusion, international law and English law should still be regarded as existing on separate planes, and international law can only become part of English law through parliamentary law-making.

Examiner's Comments:

Overall: This is a very solid attempt at handling this niche question. The candidate has shown a good level of understanding in terms of the interaction between international law and domestic law and the constitutional issues involved. This is a rather technical question that requires a good understanding of international law and parliament sovereignty so might not be for everyone. There is good evidence of analysing the types of international law involved and good examples were given with relation to the different types of conventions that the UK may be a signatory to. Overall, this essay would score an **8** or **9**.

Introduction: Good, clear introduction setting out the main arguments that will be put forward. Concise and provides a good roadmap for the examiner to follow the candidate's line of thought.

Main Body: Very good analysis of the constitutional principles behind how international law and English law may be on separate planes altogether. Maybe a comparison with EU law might have given this essay even higher marks to contrast the different levels of supremacy of law and how a sovereign state may submit to a different jurisdiction, and the difference between the presence of a central law-making authority and the absence of one (in international law).

Conclusion: Very good and succinct conclusion that summarises the argument being put forward by the candidate. There is no right or wrong answer for this question and examiners will be satisfied to see that the candidate has sufficiently argued for his or her main argument and has provided relevant evidence and explanation in order to arrive at a conclusion.

Worse response:

The UK is a global superpower and consequently must abide by international rules in order to maintain its clout in the world stage. Hence, the UK cannot just adhere to English law and not refer to international law standards. The UK is heavily interdependent on the world economy and must abide by trade rules, international standards and establish a good rapport with its neighbouring countries.

For example, the UK (at the time being) is still a member of the EU, and this clearly shows that international law standards are relevant and binding on the UK besides just English law. English law may be the dominant law for domestic issues and national matters, but international law and EU law governs matters that have an international cross-border element such as the free movement of goods and persons.

The UK is also a party to the Paris Convention. The withdrawal of the US and the ensuing backlash shows how important it is for the UK to be a party to an international convention that establishes common standards in important issues such as climate change, and for the UK to respect such standards instead of sticking to its domestic laws.

It is also the case that UK citizens are increasingly mobile and many of them are based abroad. Hence, the UK cannot just rely on domestic law to govern the rights of such people. International law standards are put in place to ensure that a common standard is enforced and situations where multiple jurisdictions are involved will be resolved by international courts. Hence, international law is becoming increasingly relevant in this globalised world and cannot be ignored.

In summary, international law is becoming an increasingly more significant part of English law as globalisation accelerates.

Examiner's Comments:

Overall: This is a potentially good essay which raised some good points. For example, international trade standards, involvement of international courts in disputes between countries and political pressure involved in the membership of certain important conventions. However, the execution is not as smooth as the previous essay. This essay shows a lower level of understanding of the constitutional principles and the interaction between English law and international law that this question is ultimately aimed at. Hence, this essay would score an above average mark of 6 to 7.

Introduction: This introduction is pretty good and reflects early on the potential of the essay by raising some important points. It could be improved by also stating the other arguments that will be raised instead of overly focusing on one aspect. It is also a little too informal with use of words like "clout". The candidate must remember that this is a formal piece of writing and only formal language should be used. The essay is also rather short which signals to the examiner that the points might not have been fully developed.

Main Body: The potential of the essay is not fully met in the analysis and explanations shown as the candidate does not go deep enough in attempt to provide a legal analysis of the exact question asked – namely the legal relationship between international law and English law. There are some very good examples raised such as the membership of the Paris Convention and the political pressure involved. It also mentions the example of EU law (with some minor imprecision with regards to the legal relationship). This essay could have achieved a much higher mark if there was more accurate and incisive legal analysis.

Conclusion: Conclusion is short and perhaps more structure marks could have been achieved by providing a good summary of the key arguments raised in order to wrap up the essay.

EXAMPLE ESSAY 12

It may be argued that fighting crime would be made very much easier if everyone was required to have their DNA registered, so that DNA found at the scene of a crime could always be matched to an individual. Would you support such a change in the law? If not, is it justifiable to register anyone's DNA, and, if so, on what grounds?

Better response:

This essay will argue against a requirement to have everyone register their DNA. While the statement correctly identifies that fighting crime will be made easier, this does not outweigh the strong arguments against such a law. First, such a change could largely be considered an infringement of our privacy. Second, instead of combating racial discrimination, such a database is likely to help perpetuate racial discrimination. Third, the limitations of DNA testing could lead to an increase in wrongful arrests.

Advantages of mandatory DNA registration

As identified in the question, the requirement for every citizen to register their DNA will help increase the speed in which suspects are identified leading to an increase in efficiency and cost. As research indicates, searching the database to find a DNA profile match helps identify around 60% of cases in the UK. Furthermore, information can be shared between databases held in different countries to identify criminals who commit crimes in more than one country or track those who have fled to another country. It could also help identify missing people and unidentifiable remains and help reunite families.

Infringement of privacy

However, these are limited advantages which do not outweigh my main argument which is that it infringes an individual's right to privacy. There are currently no comprehensive privacy regulations which ensure that the government delete the sample after a certain amount of time or prevent governments from sharing the DNA profiles with other groups such as insurance companies or commercial companies. This means the such information can be easily misused.

While some may argue that individuals already provide their own personal information to the private sector in exchange for certain services and therefore should be able to trust this information with the government, it should be noted that this was done voluntarily. If this law is implemented, an individual has no choice whether their DNA is included in the national database. As this database could be used or accessed for purposes for which the data was never originally intended, individual consent is important.

Moreover, the information provided to private sector companies is and can be limited while information found in DNA is much more extensive. Information about hair colour, eye colour, race and genetic diseases can all be found in our DNA. If such private information is shared with commercial companies, they can easily exploit this information for profit such as specifically advertising their health products to those with certain genetic diseases.

Racial discrimination
Some argue that including the whole population could eliminate ethic and gender bias for example, towards young black men. For example, police can automatically screen through the database to objectively identify the suspect rather than operate on racial assumptions. However, rather than decrease racial discrimination, I argue that this law will continue to perpetuate or worsen racial stereotypes. As proved in the David Lammy Report 2020, discrimination within the justice system in the UK has only improved marginally over the past decade. Therefore, there is a possibility that the police force would be susceptible to pursuing crimes committed by members of the overrepresented groups. The police can easily identify those from these backgrounds through their DNA. These DNA records are linked to other computer records and could also be used to deny someone a visa or job.

Limitations of DNA testing

Lastly, there is little evidence to support the fact that more crimes would be solved if everyone were to register their DNA. The increase in samples increase the chances of false matches being made and innocent people being arrested. In 2012, an innocent man was a partial match for DNA found on a murder victim. Although he had a strong alibi, he was jailed before he could prove otherwise. He was later acquitted after it was discovered that he was a taxi driver with a rare skin condition which meant that his skin flaked more often than usual. This meant that his DNA could have transferred from his taxi via money or another person onto the victim. The experience was described as very traumatising and wrongful. Such situations would inevitably increase if such a law was implemented. It could lead to further dissatisfaction and distrust in the justice system.

In conclusion, without proper privacy regulations in place, such a change should not be implemented. Even with tight security regulations, there has to be strict enforcement seen. This will not be easy to achieve and even then, the right to privacy outweighs the need for a national DNA database. The additional consequence of increased discrimination is also undesirable. As argued, there has not been enough research in the field to prove that a national DNA database will largely improve crime statistics.

Examiner's Comments:

Overall: This is a very good and clear attempt at this question. The candidate has answered all parts of the question and shown a good level of understanding of the different arguments for and against DNA testing. This is a rather general question that does not require any law knowledge. While it may be perceived as easier than technical questions, it is arguably harder to write well and impress the examiner. The threshold for a good answer to a very general question is likely higher than for a technical question as many candidates would be able to produce a coherent response. Overall, this essay would score a 7 or 8.

Introduction: The introduction makes their position clear and sets out the main arguments that will be put forward. It is concise and provides a good roadmap for the examiner to follow the candidate's line of thought.

Main Body: Very good analysis of the main arguments (infringement of privacy and racial discrimination). This is a balanced essay as the candidate recognises throughout the advantages of DNA testing while defending her position. There is good development of the arguments put forward.

Conclusion: Very good and succinct conclusion that summarises the argument being put forward by the candidate – there is no right or wrong answer for this question and examiners will be satisfied to see that the candidate has sufficiently argued for his or her main argument and has provided relevant evidence and explanation in order to arrive at a final conclusion.

Worse response:

I think that fighting crime would be very much easier if everyone was required to have their DNA registered. Hence, it is always justifiable to register anyone's DNA.

Having a database of everyone's DNA would be a very powerful tool as it can help identify the suspect quickly. The information can be used as strong evidence to demonstrate the individual's guilt.

This database would save a lot of time and money. For example, if DNA found at the crime cannot be identified quickly it would cost investigators more to find out whose DNA it is and delay the outcome of the whole case. If everyone was registered, it would only take a simple search to identify the suspect.

Although there is the argument that DNA found at the crime scene is not immediately conclusive, the benefits of the whole system outweigh the cons.

Moreover, it could also be shared between different databases held in different countries to help identify criminals who commit crimes in more than one country.

Furthermore, it could help identify missing individuals. This DNA database is useful for fighting crime but also has other uses.

In summary, everyone should get their DNA registered to help solve crime faster and save costs.

Examiner's Comments:

Overall: This is an underdeveloped essay which raised some good points such as efficiency and sharing between different databases. It also attempts to balance their essay by identifying that DNA found at the crime scene is not always conclusive evidence. However, the execution is not as smooth as the previous essay. This essay also does not mention the main argument against this statement which is infringement of privacy. Hence, this essay would score a mark of 2 to 3.

Introduction: This introduction sets out their position. It could be improved by also stating the other arguments that will be raised. While first person is not marked down, as this is an academic piece of writing third person is preferred.

Main Body: The potential of the essay is not fully met in the analysis and explanations shown as the candidate does not go deep enough in attempt to provide a legal analysis of the exact question asked. The candidate tries to balance the essay but fails to argue convincingly that the benefits of the system outweigh the disadvantages. There is also use of informal language like "con" which is not preferred in an academic piece of writing. There are some good points raised but they were very underdeveloped. The candidate has made their point but the explanation and evidence was lacking. This essay could have achieved a much higher mark if there was more accurate and incisive analysis.

Conclusion: Conclusion is short and perhaps more structure marks could have been achieved by providing a good summary of the key arguments raised in order to wrap up the essay.

EXAMPLE ESSAY 13

Should a drug dealer ever be punished for the death of someone who overdoses on drugs that he has supplied?

Better response:

This essay will argue that a drug dealer should not be punished for the death of someone who overdoses except if they have a prior relationship such as spouse or familial ties. I will define 'drugs' as hard or recreational drugs which are non-medicinal. I will also interpret being 'punished for the death' as being charged for murder. First, the overdose could be due to several other factors which could be irrelevant or not have been foreseen by the drug dealer. Second, due to the inelastic demand for drugs, a potential murder charge is unlikely to be a deterrent. Third, this punishment has the potential effect of unfairly marginalising the most vulnerable in society.

<u>*Drug dealers should be punished*</u>

It has been long established that those with a prior relationship to the victim are responsible for the welfare of the dependent. This means that is an obligation for siblings, spouses or those with close familial ties to ensure that those under their care do not engage in activity which may harm them. Thus, those who allow overdose would be responsible. However, this is a very limited category of people.

There are several other arguments that support punishing a drug dealer with no prior relationship to the victim for the death of an overdose. First, imposing such a harsh punishment could function as a deterrent. Those thinking of coming into the market and even those who already are within the trade might decide to exit the market in fear of being labelled a murderer. Such harsh punishment functions as a strong signalling function in society to condemn the drug trade. However, as explained in depth below, drugs have an inelastic demand therefore imposing a harsh punishment is unlikely to produce such a deterrent effect.

Second, it has a strong retributive effect. In the US, there has been growing favour to charge drug dealers with murder. This is because it is "justice being done" for victims and their families. This is particularly attractive given the rising death toll due to drug overdose in countries like the US. However, this will be argued to be a violation of the proportionality principle.

While an overdose victim's death can be as tragic as one who got stabbed, a drug supplier cannot be considered the same as a murderer. Supplying drugs can be considered, at most, a minor offence compared to first-degree murder which could result in life imprisonment. As explained later, an imposition of such a disproportionate punishment only serves to marginalise vulnerable groups.

Drug dealers should not be punished
There are persuasive reasons why drug dealers should not be charged with murder. First, the issue of causation. It is not easy to establish that the sole cause of the overdose was the drugs supplied by the dealer. Drug users often take a mixture of substances at once or engage in other activities such as drinking alcohol which could all contribute to the eventual overdose. It would be very difficult – and unfair – to attribute the cause to one drug dealer who supplied some drugs. It is not reasonable for every drug dealer to predict the risk profile of their own product or what other substances the drug user would take with their product. Thus, it would be illogical to charge one drug dealer (or multiple) with a murder charge.

Second, there is no data proving that this would be an effective deterrent. In fact, due to the inelastic demand, it is unlikely to be a deterrent. The black market for drugs would continue to exist and grow regardless of such impositions due to inelastic demand. Therefore, such an inappropriate and disproportionate punishment would only serve to further marginalise those who resorted to the trade due to financial difficulty and risk mislabelling the vulnerable. These tend to be people of colour which only fuels further racism within the justice system. As the justice system is still very racism, it further serves to perpetuate and create worse stereotypes for the weakest in society.

It could also have the effect of causing more deaths as it discourages people from calling 911 for help since every overdose scene would be treated as a crime scene. The benefits of saving a life of an overdose arguable outweighs any retributive, deterrent or criminal justice rationale.

Conclusion. To conclude, drug dealers should not be unjustly mislabelled as murderers given the detrimental societal impact. Not only is the punishment disproportionate, it is inappropriate given the difficulty in establishing causation and it might have the reverse effect. There are many better ways of punishing those who illegally sell drugs which have been evidentially proven and rather measures should be taken to help alleviate these people out of the black market rather than vindicate them further.

Examiner's Comments:

Overall: This is a very good attempt at a more general question. The candidate has used headings and definitions to ensure that the examiner is on the same page as them and that their arguments make sense. The ability to identify parts of the question and define them is an important skill for law students. The candidate is signalling to the examiner that they will be a good law student. There is good discussion the types of arguments and good examples were given. Overall, this essay would score a 7 or 8.

Introduction: The introduction makes their position clear and sets out the main arguments that will be put forward. It is concise and provides a good roadmap for the examiner to follow the candidate's line of thought.

Main Body: The use of headings makes it easy for the examiner to identify the candidate's arguments. Headings are not used typically in A Level essays but are favoured in Cambridge Law Essays. It makes it very clear what the paragraph is about. It would impress the examiner and aid your structure if you use headings. This is a balanced essay as the candidate analyses reasons why drug dealers should or should not be punished. The arguments are well developed and defended. The candidate uses good examples (the US) and identifies principles like proportionality and causation.

Conclusion: Very good and succinct conclusion that summarises the argument being put forward by the candidate – there is no right or wrong answer for this question and examiners will be satisfied to see that the candidate has sufficiently argued for his or her main argument and has provided relevant evidence and explanation in order to arrive at a final conclusion.

Worse response:

Drug dealers should not be punished for the death of those who overdose on drugs. It is not fair to punish drug dealers as the customers know what they are getting into and drug dealers cannot enforce or police how much they take. It is purely a business transaction and it would be unjust to hold them liable as people could take a mixture of substances.

It is hard to identify the cause of death and to say that it was the drug dealer's fault. A person might take a mixture of substances and it is hard to say that one substance caused the death. People could buy different substances from different drug dealers so how do we identify which drug dealer is at fault?

This is different if the drug dealer has a relationship of trust and dependency with the customer and supplier. If the drug dealer is your sister, then they could be at fault if they don't ensure you take it responsibly. This is because your sister could have a duty of care towards you.

Moreover, if the argument is that raising the punishment to death will have a deterrent effect this is wrong. As the demand for drugs is inelastic, raising the punishment will not decrease demand or supply. Drugs are illegal but the availability of drugs on the market has still increased in present day. If there is demand, product supply and labour supply will always be filled by new entrants so punishing them will not deter them. In summary, drug dealers should not be punished for the death of someone who overdosed on drugs that they have supplied.

Examiner's Comments:

Overall: This is an underdeveloped essay. It feels rushed and shows the examiner that the candidate did not properly think through how to structure the essay. It feels more like the candidate ran out of time and just tried to put something down on the page. While the points raised are good, there is not enough critical analysis. It attempts to balance their essay by raising points for the argument that they should be punished but it feels haphazard. Hence, this essay would score a mark of 3 to 4.

Introduction: This introduction sets out their position which is good. It could be improved by also stating the other arguments that will be raised. While it is a good start, it starts to go into the substantive body which is not advised.

Main Body: The potential of the essay is not fully met in the analysis and explanations shown as the candidate does not go deep enough in attempt to provide a legal analysis of the exact question asked. The candidate tries to balance the essay but fails to develop any of their arguments. There is also use of rhetorical question which is not advised. You should make solid arguments backed up with good examples. There are some good points raised but they were very underdeveloped. The candidate has rushed through writing it – they might have spent too long planning the essay and left too little time to writing. This essay could have achieved a much higher mark if there was more accurate and incisive analysis.

Conclusion: Conclusion is rather short and does not add any value to the essay. It feels like an afterthought and doesn't summarise the arguments well.

FINAL ADVICE

GIVE YOURSELF ENOUGH TIME

The CLT is usually done in college (or online due to COVID-19) and might be done right before an interview. It is important to make sure you give yourself adequate time beforehand to prepare for the CLT and read up as much about legal issues as you can. When you travel to Cambridge for the interview and CLT, things may get rather overwhelming with the new environment and administrative matters you have to settle, hence make sure you are sufficiently prepared so you can attempt the test with confidence!

PLAN PROPERLY

It bears repeating that a good structure and adequate planning beforehand goes a long way – you have one hour to do an essay question, choose **wisely** and only attempt a question if you feel confident that you fully understand what is being asked, and make sure you have sufficient points to make in order to write a good essay with a good level of legal analysis.

HOW THE CLT WILL BE USED

Remember – the CLT is used in conjunction with many different elements to determine whether you get an offer or not – be it the personal statement, interview, or any extra marked written work that may be requested by your college. You want to maximise your chances of getting an offer by doing well in all elements, so make sure you take the time to prepare for the CLT on top of preparing for the interview!

AFTERWORD

Getting a place to study law in Cambridge is undeniably tough, but it is achievable if you are truly passionate about studying law and work hard in doing your best in preparing for the CLT. This is also a good way of finding out if you are truly interested in studying law as an academic subject, as you should find your preparation enjoyable and the content interesting and thought-provoking.

Good luck!

ABOUT US

We currently publish over 85 titles across a range of subject areas – covering specialised admissions tests, examination techniques, personal statement guides, plus everything else you need to improve your chances of getting on to competitive courses such as medicine and law, as well as into universities such as Oxford and Cambridge.

Outside of publishing we also operate a highly successful tuition division, called UniAdmissions. This company was founded in 2013 by Dr Rohan Agarwal and Dr David Salt, both Cambridge Medical graduates with several years of tutoring experience. Since then, every year, hundreds of applicants and schools work with us on our programmes. Through the programmes we offer, we deliver expert tuition, exclusive course places, online courses, best-selling textbooks and much more.

With a team of over 1,000 Oxbridge tutors and a proven track record, UniAdmissions have quickly become the UK's number one admissions company.

Visit and engage with us at:

Website (UniAdmissions): www.uniadmissions.co.uk

Facebook: www.facebook.com/uniadmissionsuk

YOUR FREE BOOK

Thanks for purchasing this Ultimate Book. Readers like you have the power to make or break a book —hopefully you found this one useful and informative. *UniAdmissions* would love to hear about your experiences with this book. As thanks for your time we'll send you another eBook from our Ultimate Guide series absolutely <u>FREE</u>!

How to Redeem Your Free eBook

1) Find the book you have on your Amazon
purchase history or your email receipt to help find the book on Amazon.

2) On the product page at the Customer Reviews area, click 'Write a customer review'. Write your review and post it! Copy the review page or take a screen shot of the review you have left.

3) Head over to www.uniadmissions.co.uk/free-book and select your chosen free eBook!

Your eBook will then be emailed to you – it's as simple as that!
Alternatively, you can buy all the titles at

Printed by Amazon Italia Logistica S.r.l.
Torrazza Piemonte (TO), Italy

43396578R00083